THAMES VA

Teashop W

THAMES VALLEY
Teashop Walks

Jean Patefield

COUNTRYSIDE BOOKS
NEWBURY BERKSHIRE

First published 1998
© Jean Patefield 1998
Revised and updated 2002, 2008

COUNTRYSIDE BOOKS
3 Catherine Road
Newbury, Berkshire

ISBN 978 1 85306 547 7

To view our complete range of books,
please visit us at
www.countrysidebooks.co.uk

Designed by Graham Whiteman
Cover illustration by Colin Doggett
Photographs and maps by the author

Produced through MRM Associates Ltd., Reading
Typeset by Techniset Typesetters, Newton-le-Willows
Printed by Cambridge University Press

*All material for the manufacture of this book
was sourced from sustainable forests.*

Contents

Walk

KEY TO SKETCH MAPS

Path on route	— → —	Other rivers	∿∿∿	Pub referred to in text	PH
Path not on route	...	Lake		Point in text	⑤
Road	══	Church	†	Car park	☐
River Thames	∼ ∼ ∼	Teashop		Isolated building referred to in text	▬

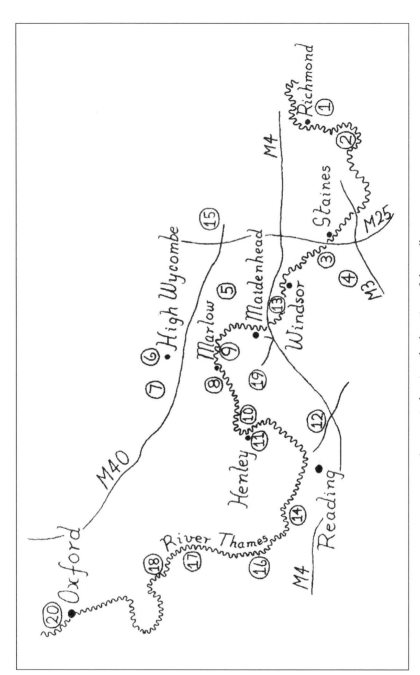

Area map showing the location of the walks.

Introduction

'The River,' corrected the Rat.
'And you really live by the River? What a jolly life!'
'By it and with it or on it and in it,' said the Rat. 'It's brothers and sisters to me, and aunts, and company, and food, and drink and (naturally) washing. It's my world and I don't want any other. What it hasn't got is not worth having, and what it doesn't know, is not worth knowing.'

Tens of thousands would agree with Kenneth Grahame's view in *The Wind in the Willows* and return again and again to the banks of the Thames to walk, fish, mess about in boats or simply to count the ducklings.

This is England's greatest river and its gentle, pastoral appearance belies its force for most of its length. Only at Goring Gap, where it slices through the chalk to separate the Berkshire Downs from the Chiltern Hills, does it hint at the power that can deliver billions of gallons of water a day across Teddington Lock. For most of its course it is a sleeping giant, meandering through the countryside as it falls gently to the sea at an average rate of 20 inches a mile.

For centuries the Thames was both a barrier to communication and an important highway. Important towns grew up at crossing points such as at Wallingford, once second only to Winchester with its own mint. Today we do not think of peaceful riverside towns such as Marlow and Henley as ports but that was their former role, exporting timber and other products downriver to London. The important link with London has made the banks of the river popular with monarchs who have traditionally had their country retreats by the Thames at Richmond, Hampton and Windsor so there is history in abundance along the way.

This mass of water has not always remained confined in its course in an orderly manner. For centuries flooding has been a serious problem and many towns are therefore centred somewhat away from the river. Only in recent years has this been ameliorated somewhat by modern river management: there have been boats in the streets of Maidenhead in living memory.

Towards the end of the 19th century messing about in boats on the river became an immensely popular pastime. Jerome K. Jerome's famous book, *Three Men in a Boat*, was published in 1889 and sold two million copies in the author's lifetime. This hilarious story of the three clerks' trip on the Thames added yet further to its popularity.

Before mechanical power arrived, barges drawn by men or horses transported people and goods on the river. Due to natural obstacles and unco-operative landowners, the towpath had to cross the river many times. Since the 1920s there has been support for using the redundant towpath as a long distance route and the Thames Path is now a reality. It follows the river for 180 miles from its source in Gloucestershire to the Thames Barrier at Woolwich and many of the walks in this book make use of it.

These 20 walks explore the Thames Valley between Richmond and Oxford. They do not stick rigidly to the riverside, though many do include a stretch along one bank or the other, but also explore the delightful countryside on either side, which includes parts of the Chilterns and the Berkshire Downs. They are all between $2\frac{1}{2}$ and $8\frac{1}{2}$ miles long and should be well within the capacity of the average person, including those of mature years and families with children. They are intended to take the walker through this attractive corner of England at a gentle pace with plenty of time to stop and stare, to savour the beauty and interest all around. A dedicated yomper and stomper could probably knock off the whole book in a single weekend but in doing so they would have missed the point and seen nothing. To fully appreciate the countryside it is necessary to go slowly with your eyes and ears open.

Some of the walks are short and level, ideal for a pipe opener on a winter's day, or giving plenty of time to idle by the river in summer, watching the birds and the boats. Others are longer or more strenuous, some making an excellent all-day expedition. Certain of the walks involve some climbing. This is inevitable as hills add enormous interest to the countryside and with no hills there are no views. However, this presents no problem to the sensible walker who has three uphill gears - slowly, very slowly and admiring the view. None of the walks in this book are inherently hazardous but sensible care should be taken. Many of the falls that do happen are due to unsuitable footwear, particularly unridged soles since grass slopes can be as slippery as the more obviously hazardous wet, smooth rock. Proper walking shoes or boots also give some protection to the ankle. It is also essential to look where you are putting your feet to avoid tripping up. Wainwright, the doyen of walkers in the Lake District, said that he never had a serious fall in all his years and thousands of miles of walking because he always looked where he put his feet and stopped if he wanted to admire the scenery.

All the routes are on public rights of way or permissive paths and have been carefully checked but, of course, in the countryside things do change; a gate is replaced by a stile or a wood is extended. Each walk is circular and is illustrated by a sketch map. An Ordnance Survey map is useful as well, especially for identifying the main features of views. The area is covered by Explorer map numbers 159, 160, 161, 170, 171, 172 and 180. The grid reference of the starting point and the number of the appropriate Explorer sheet are given for each walk.

The walks are designed so that, starting where suggested, the teashop is reached in the second half so a really good appetite for tea can be worked up and then its effects walked off. Some walks start at a car park, which is ideal. Where this is not possible, the suggested starting place will always have somewhere where a few cars can be left without endangering other traffic or causing inconvenience. However, it sometimes fits in better with the plans for the day to start and finish at the teashop and so for each walk there are details of how to do this.

Tea is often said to be the best meal to eat out in England and I believe that it is something to be enjoyed on all possible occasions. Scones with cream and strawberry jam, delicious home-made cakes, toasted teacakes dripping with butter in winter, delicate cucumber sandwiches in summer, all washed down with the cup that cheers. Bad for the figure maybe, but the walking will see to that.

The best teashops serve a range of cakes, all home-made and including fruit cake as well as scones and other temptations. Teapots should be capacious and pour properly. Most of the teashops visited on these walks fulfil these criteria admirably and they all offer a good tea. They always have at least light lunches available as well so there is no need to think of these walks as just something for the afternoons.

The pleasures of summer walking are obvious. Many of the teashops featured in this book have an attractive garden where tea can be taken outside when the weather is suitable. However, let me urge you not to overlook the pleasures of a good walk in winter. The roads and paths are quieter and what could be better than sitting by an open fire in a cosy teashop scoffing crumpets that you can enjoy with a clear conscience due to the brisk walk to get them!

Teashops are not scattered evenly throughout the Thames Valley. In some places popular with tourists, the visitor is spoilt for choice. In such cases the most convenient teashop that, in the author's opinion, most closely fulfils the criteria set out above is recommended but should that not appeal, there are others from which to choose. In other places where there is a delightful walk to be enjoyed, the choice for tea may be more limited. However, they all offer a good tea partway round an attractive walk. The opening times and telephone number of each teashop are given. Some are rather vague about when they open out of season: it seems to depend on weather and mood. If you are planning a walk on a wet November

Tuesday, for example, a call to check that tea will actually be available that day is a wise precaution. A few are definitely closed in the depths of winter and for these walks an alternative source of refreshment is given. In most cases, these are pubs serving food which in some cases includes tea.

So put on your walking shoes and prepare to be delighted, by the charms of the countryside near England's mightiest river and a traditional English tea!

Jean Patefield

Walk 1
RICHMOND HILL

*A*bove all else, this is a walk for a clear day! To the west, Richmond Hill has a steep scarp slope above the Thames near Teddington, the tidal limit of the river. From the summit, there are magnificent, panoramic views over the Thames Valley, and the location of many other walks in this book. More surprising is the view east, the famous vista of St Paul's 10 miles away. This outstanding viewpoint is backed by Richmond Park, an exceptionally attractive expanse of grassland studded with woodland and ponds. Walking in this green oasis, it is almost impossible to believe you are so near one of the world's great cities. The views are attained with almost no perceptible climbing making this a very easy walk and highly recommended.

Pembroke Lodge is the high spot, both literally and figuratively, of Richmond Park. Tea can be taken in the elegant rooms inside or on the extensive terrace, both with the same stunning views. There is musical entertainment on the patio in the afternoon on summer weekends. A selection of cakes and gateaux is served, with an especially good range of doughnuts, and cream teas with clotted cream. For lunch there are tasty sandwiches and filled jacket potatoes or, for a fuller meal, a daily choice of hot meals, such as gammon with cider and pineapple sauce. Pembroke Lodge is open from 10 am throughout the year, closing at 4 pm in winter and 5.30 pm in summer. Please note that dogs other than guide dogs are not allowed in the gardens in which Pembroke Lodge is situated. Telephone: 0181 9408207.

DISTANCE: 4 miles.
MAP: OS Explorer 161 London South.
STARTING POINT: Sheen Gate car park, Richmond Park (GR 204744).
HOW TO GET THERE: From the A205 (the South Circular road) Upper Richmond Road at East Sheen SW14 turn down Sheen Lane to Sheen Gate into Richmond Park and the car park is just beyond on the right.
ALTERNATIVE STARTING POINT: If you wish to visit the teashop at the beginning or end of your walk, start at Pembroke Lodge car park, accessed from Richmond Gate (GR 186729). You will then start the walk at point 9, turning left along the top of the slope.

THE WALK

1. Return to the entrance to the car park and take a path behind a notice board. After 5 yards take the left-hand of three paths. Cross a major path and continue to an enclosed wood.

This is Two Storms Wood, planted in 1993/4 to replace the trees lost in the great storms of 1987 and 1990. The high gate and fence are to keep the deer out until the trees are fully established.

2. Go through a gate and follow the main path ahead to another gate.

3. Continue on the main path, ignoring paths on the left leading towards a road. The path soon has a wire fence on the right. When the fence ends at gates and a drive, continue along the drive, passing the entrance to Holly Lodge.

4. At the end of a wooden fence on the right, turn right onto grass.

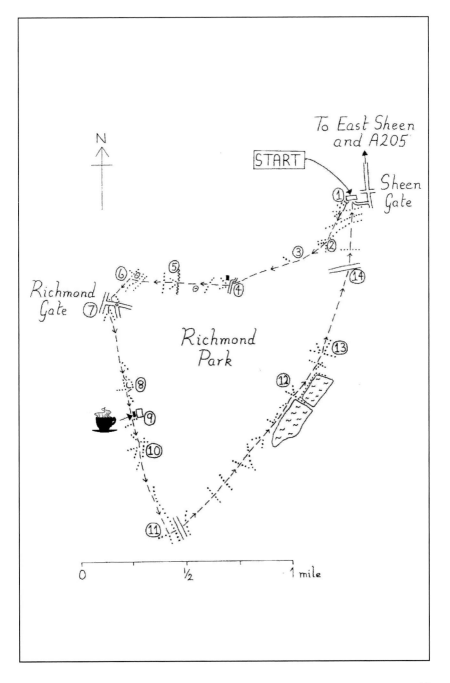

N
↑

To East Sheen
and A205

START

Sheen
Gate

① ②
③
⑤
⑥ ④
Richmond
Gate ⑦
⑭
⑬
Richmond
Park
⑧ ⑫
⑨
⑩
⑪

0   ½   1 mile

At this point, there are three grassy paths ahead. Take the centre one, towards trees. Ignore all cross paths and pass to the right of a pond into a wood.

The stretch of the Thames from Kew to Windsor has traditionally been the site of country homes for the kings and queens of England, conveniently situated by the important highway that was the river. A Norman manor at Richmond, or Shene as it was then called, grew into a Plantagenet palace. Henry VII built a new palace, called Richmond because he was Duke of Richmond before he became king, and he died here as did his granddaughter, Elizabeth I. The hunting grounds were enclosed by Charles I. During the Civil War Richmond Palace was damaged by the Parliamentarians and later declined in favour of Hampton Court (see walk 2) and Windsor, so little remains today. The park was given to the City of London then returned to the crown at the Restoration. Today, it is the largest of the royal parks and a wonderful lung for the city.

5. Immediately after crossing a small stream, by a huge fallen tree, the path forks into three: take the centre one. At the edge of the trees, head across the open grass, going to the right of a clump of six trees. Cross a horse trail and go by a pond to a major path beyond.

6. Turn left and walk to Richmond Gate. Cross the road to a notice board.

Just outside Richmond Gate is the Star and Garter Home for disabled servicemen, built in the 1920s on the site of a famous tavern where Dickens loved to celebrate family anniversaries and the publication of his novels.

7. Turn left along a surfaced path with a metal fence on the right. Go through a gate into Pembroke Lodge Gardens and walk along the main path ahead. At the end of the Laburnum Walk, take the centre one of three paths to the view point.
   Note: dogs are not allowed in the gardens so walkers with dogs must bear left round the garden to rejoin the route at point 10.

The view from Henry VIII's Mound is the climax of this walk. The Mound is probably a prehistoric barrow and its evolution is explained on a nearby notice board. Be sure to go right up to the top of the Mound where there are some lines quoted from James Thomson's 'The Seasons', written in 1727; you may have noticed a memorial to him on the right as you entered the gardens. They are still apt today. The panoramic view to the west is outstanding and includes the location of several other walks in this book. Nearby are Hampton Court and Bushy Park (walk 2). The distance to Runnymede, visited on walk 3, is given on the plaque illustrating the main features of the view. The hills beyond are the lovely Chilterns, the site of walks 6, 7, 8 and 16. Also in view is Twickenham, the home of English rugby. Through a metal arch at the rear is the famous vista to St Paul's, one of the most significant views in the capital and protected by law. The Mound is said to get its name from the fact that Henry VIII was here when news came that Anne Boleyn had been executed. When you visit Hampton Court, you will be told that he was playing tennis there: in fact, he was probably miles away in Wiltshire. The prosaic truth is more likely to be that he used to stand on this hill while deer were driven past for him to shoot.

8. After admiring the view, follow the path down the other side of the Mound then turn right to continue along the main path through the gardens, always bearing right to stay on top of the slope, to Pembroke Lodge.

The view from Richmond Hill.

Pembroke Lodge dates back to the 18th century when it was a mole catcher's cottage. William III died after falling from his horse in Kensington after it stumbled over a mole hill so a mole catcher was employed to make sure the hunting ground was free of dangerous mole hills. It was extended for Elizabeth, Countess of Pembroke in 1788 then granted to the Prime Minister, Lord Russell, in 1848. It remained in the Russell family until the 1940s and the famous philosopher Bertrand Russell spent his childhood here.

9. After tea, continue through the garden in the same direction. When the tarmac path bends left, continue ahead on a gravelled path for 20 yards to a gate.

10. Through the gate, carry on in the same direction on any of the paths for nearly ½ mile, staying roughly parallel with the road and being careful not to stray too far to the right downhill, until you reach a broad crossing path much used by horses. (Note: if you come to a metalled road you have gone about 250 yards too far and must retrace your steps.)

There are many ancient oaks in Richmond Park. Were it not for human activities, much of England would be covered by oak forests. There would be many other types of trees and shrubs growing alongside the oaks but they would be the dominant tree. As our most important native species, oaks are of immense ecological importance and support more varieties of animals than any other. It has been estimated that some 300 species of invertebrates feed only on oak while another 1,200 get some of their food from this source. These creatures are then themselves eaten by others, which can thus be said to depend on the oak.

11. Turn left on the cross path to a road. Cross the road and go straight ahead on a clear path, soon crossing a sanded horse trail. Ignore all cross paths and continue ahead to a large pond on the right.

You will be very unfortunate if you do not see deer during your walk. There are estimated to be about 600 deer in the park. They are fallow deer, which are not truly native to Britain. Remains have been found in deposits from before the last Ice Age but they died out when the ice came and did not make it back before the rising waters of the Channel cut Britain off from the rest of Europe. They are believed to have been reintroduced by the Normans for food and hunting.

The small mounds seen in many places in the park, but particularly to the right of this path, are ant hills. They are a sign that the ground has not been disturbed for a long time. The growing conditions on the mounds are a little different to the surrounding ground, being warmer and drier, so they tend to support a slightly different flora. You will also notice that many mounds are crowned with rabbit droppings. These are deposited by male rabbits to help mark their territory.

12. At the end of the first pond cross a broad track and continue in the same direction. The path is much fainter now and there is a second, smaller pond some 50 yards away on the right. At the end of the second pond, continue close to trees on the left to a broad cross path.

13. From here the path is not visible on the ground. Look for a building with a red roof and a chimney about ½ mile ahead in trees. Head across the grass towards this building until you intersect a road.

14. Cross the road and adjacent cycle track to pick up a faint grassy path, now heading to the left of the chimney, which belongs to the gatehouse at Sheen Gate. This leads back to the car park.

Walk 2
HAMPTON COURT

Hampton Court was Queen Anne's favourite summer palace and is where the poet Pope satirizes her in 'The Rape of the Lock':

Here Thou, great Anna!
whom three realms obey,
Dost sometimes counsel take -
and sometimes Tea.

On this walk we can emulate the monarch and take tea at Hampton Court. The route itself is not long and is easy, level going but plenty of time should be allowed to visit the many features of this historic place. There are even more just off the route and these can easily be found using the maps displayed throughout the gardens. Some of the level walking is across parkland where you are almost certain to see herds of deer. There is a

stretch by the Thames and the route also crosses some of the formal gardens round the great palace. A charge is made for visiting the buildings but entrance to the park and gardens is free.

The delightful Tiltyard Tearooms have a large, airy interior and plenty of tables outside overlooking attractive gardens. A tempting array of cakes and desserts is on offer as well as cream teas with clotted cream. For lunch, there is a daily hot selection as well as tasty salads and filled baguettes. Open from 10 am throughout the year, closing about 4.30 pm in winter and 6 pm in summer. Telephone: 0181 9433666.

DISTANCE: 4¹/₂ miles.
MAP: OS Explorer 161 London South.
STARTING POINT: Car park by the Diana Fountain in Bushy Park (GR 160693).
HOW TO GET THERE: Enter Bushy Park by the Lion Gate entrance on Hampton Court Road, the A308, opposite the Kings Arms. The car park is on the right, just past the Diana Fountain.
ALTERNATIVE STARTING POINT: If you wish to visit the teashop at the beginning or end of your walk, start in the Trophy Gates car park at Hampton Court. Leave at the back of the car park and the tea room is to the left. You will then start the walk at point 8.

THE WALK
Note: this walk should not be attempted between mid-June and mid-July as part of the parkland crossed is used for the Hampton Court Flower Show and is therefore closed to the public.

1. From the entrance to the car park take the right-hand one of two paths on the left and make your way back to the Lion Gate entrance.

2. Cross the road to the entrance to Hampton Court Palace. Through the gate, go almost straight on, slightly left, on a surfaced path leading to a gate into a formal garden.

Each generation has had a hand in making the gardens surrounding the palace. Wolsey, Henry VIII, Charles I and II, William and Mary were all keen gardeners, served by the leading professionals of their day. One of the most famous features is the maze, not directly on the route described but signed from it. Some of its fame comes from its inclusion in Jerome K. Jerome's immortal 'Three Men in a Boat – to say nothing of the Dog' when Harris nearly causes a riot leading people through the

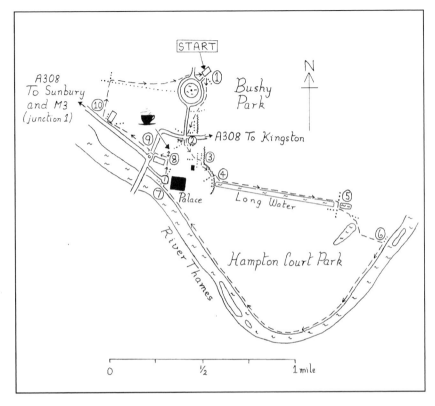

maze. *When he wrote the book Jerome thought of it as a guide to the river with some lighter passages. His editor much preferred the funny bits and it was book of the year in 1889. With the money he earned, Jerome could retire and spent the rest of his life living near the Thames, at Marlow and Ewelme.*

One of the few real tennis courts open to the public has been here since Henry VIII, who was a keen player, acquired the palace. He is said to have been playing on this court when news came of Anne Boleyn's execution. However, he is also said to have been on Richmond Hill (see walk 1) and was probably miles away in Wiltshire.

3. Go straight ahead on a gravelled path to a moat. Turn right and follow the path by the moat to a footbridge. Cross the bridge and go through a gate then follow the fence round to the right to Long Water.

This façade overlooking the magnificent gardens and with views up Long Water is the Renaissance palace built by Sir Christopher Wren for William and Mary. The original plan was to entirely demolish the Tudor palace but economy and Mary's tragic death in 1694 intervened and only the Tudor state apartments were replaced. Anne completed the work begun by her sister and brother-in-law. George II was the last monarch to live here and after his death the private apartments were converted into 'grace and favour' residences for distinguished servants of the crown. The State apartments were opened to the public by the young Queen Victoria soon after her accession.

4. Turn left to walk by Long Water to a surfaced drive.

5. Turn right, looking up Long Water for a good view of the palace. Turn left at a cross drive. After about 100 yards bear right on a grassy path to pass to the left of Rick Pond. This leads to a gate onto a fenced path to the river bank.

6. Turn right along the river bank.

7. Just after the landing stage at Hampton Court Palace, turn right into the gardens, passing in front of the Tudor façade. Continue through an archway ahead to the teashop.

Thomas Wolsey, son of an Ipswich butcher, rose to become Archbishop of York and Lord Chancellor of England as well as being made a Cardinal by the Pope. He leased the manor of Hampton Court from the Knights of St John and began to build the most magnificent private house in England. There were extensive and luxuriously furnished apartments, sufficient to accommodate the French ambassador and all his retinue when he visited in 1527 with nearly 300 courtiers. Henry VIII was jealous of this magnificence. In the hope of placating his sovereign, Wolsey presented Hampton Court to the King but this gesture was to no avail. In 1529 he was stripped of his offices and died the following year. Henry VIII took possession and the palace became a favoured residence with him and his successors. He enlarged it further and dallied here with Anne Boleyn, entwining an 'H' with an 'A' in lover's knots as part of the decoration. Scarcely was this completed before Anne fell from grace, her place taken by her lady-in-waiting, Jane Seymour, whose initials mostly replaced those of her erstwhile mistress. Queen Jane gave Henry his longed for son, the future Edward VI, and died of puerperal fever two weeks later. It is said that the prince's nurse, Mistress Penn, still walks the corridors. Henry VIII learned of the faithlessness of his fifth queen, Katherine Howard, at Hampton Court. She slipped away from her guards and ran to plead with him in the chapel while he prayed but was dragged away screaming before she could reach the

Hampton Court Palace.

royal pew. He ignored her piercing cries and her ghost too is said to haunt the palace. In the long story of Hampton Court we find Mary spending her honeymoon with Philip of Spain, James I conferring with clerics which led to the Authorised Version of the bible and Charles I fleeing house arrest by crossing the river in a wherry. William and Mary wrought great changes but, as explained above, left the exuberance of the Tudor palace which is in such contrast to the austere restraint of their Renaissance building, passed earlier. Anne drank tea here and George II entertained his mistresses Mrs Howard and Mary Bellenden. The damage caused by a fire in 1986 has been restored and the palace is well worth visiting. It is open every day from 9.30 am (10.15 am on Mondays) until 6 pm in the summer between mid-March and mid-October, closing at 4.30 pm in the winter. The last admission is 45 minutes before closing time. Telephone: 0181 7819500.

8. After tea, retrace your steps towards the archway but take the first path on the right to a road.

The teashop takes its name from Henry VIII's tiltyard where he used to joust. Around it were five towers from which spectators could watch the sport. After four of them were demolished in the 17th century, the ground was used as a kitchen garden.

24

9. Turn left for a few yards to a pedestrian crossing then head along the left-hand side of Hampton Court Green. Pass a car park and continue along the pavement for a few yards to a gate into Bushy Park.

Bushy Park has always been part of the grounds of Hampton Court. It extends to 1,100 acres and also has herds of deer, hence the tall, elaborate gates at the entrance. When William III and Wren were planning the renovations and rebuilding its layout was planned to rival Versailles. An avenue of 274 chestnuts flanked by a double row of limes was laid for a mile across the park, broken about a third of the way along to form a circle round the Diana Fountain. The exact identity of the lady is not clear, perhaps Venus or Arethusa, and the statue by Francesco Fanelli was bought in Italy for the private garden at Hampton Court by Charles I. In the north of the park, not passed on this walk, is Bushy House. This is now the home of the National Physical Laboratory but once housed William IV while he was Duke of Clarence, along with his mistress Mrs Jordan and their ten children (see walk 14).

10. Through the gate, follow the path ahead to a surfaced drive. Cross this then turn right to walk on a broad grassy path between lines of trees. As you approach the fountain, bear left, back to the start.

Walk 3
RUNNYMEDE

Many places may claim to be the centre of England but Runnymede must be its soul: it was here, in 1215, that the principle that the law is above kings and barons was negotiated and enshrined in Magna Carta. This historic site is now owned and carefully managed by the National Trust and is the setting for a charming and interesting short walk, which also literally visits the United States of America!

Magna Carta Tea Rooms, housed in a building designed by Lutyens, serve a delicious selection of cakes and other teatime goodies. For a light lunch sandwiches are always available and daily specials, which change with the seasons. Open all year. The hours vary a bit depending on the time of year but the teashop is always open between 9.30 am and 4 pm, later in the summer. Telephone: 01784 477110.

DISTANCE: 3 miles.

MAP: OS Explorer 160 Windsor, Weybridge & Bracknell.

STARTING POINT: Car park at Runnymede Pleasure Grounds (GR 008723).

HOW TO GET THERE: The starting point is on the A308 Windsor to Staines road, about 1/2 mile west of junction 13 of the M25.

ALTERNATIVE STARTING POINT: If you wish to visit the teashop at the beginning or end of your walk, start at the National Trust car park about 1/2 mile west of the Pleasure Grounds car park. The teashop is across the road. There is also a car park next to the teashop. You will then start the walk at point 8.

THE WALK

1. From the car park turn left along the main road towards Staines for about 300 yards.

2. Turn right on a signed path over a stile. After 130 yards, at an oblique cross path, branch left (do not go ahead to a gate) to a seat. Now walk with a hedge on your right to a fork then bear left. You are making for a finger post across the meadow by an area of woodland. At a second cross path, about 40 yards before the finger post, turn right to a small wooden bridge then continue to a gate on the left.

3. Do not go through the gate but bear half right to some ponds and then follow the path to the left of the ponds, passing an information board, to a gate.

4. Turn right to continue in the same direction with the ponds on your right, crossing two stiles. After the second stile follow the main path round to the right onto a board walk to a third stile.

This area has been designated a Site of Special Scientific Interest (SSSI) because of the flora and fauna of the ponds, which are home to several nationally scarce species of invertebrates. This area is rich soil carried downstream by the river and deposited in the flood plain. In the past it was ploughed up to grow crops but has now been sown with appropriate grasses and wild flowers.

5. Over the stile turn immediately left and walk along the left side of the meadows, along the bottom of Cooper's Hill, to the Magna Carta Memorial.

King John's reign was a disaster and he lost the support of the barons who forced him to sign a document granting them certain liberties and protection from

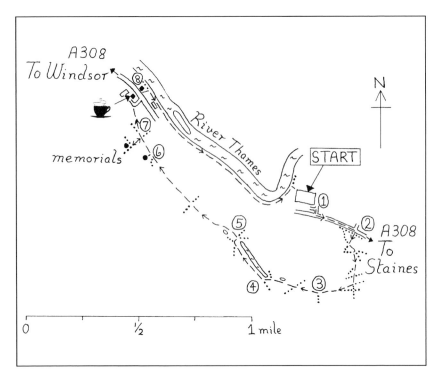

injustice. The King was staying at Windsor and the rebellious barons were encamped at Staines so Runnymede was conveniently between the two with open space for tents and armies. The ordinary people got nothing from Magna Carta - they were beneath consideration - but the document embodied the principle that the law is above all and is the precursor of our democratic rights and freedoms.

'No free man shall be...imprisoned or...outlawed...except by the lawful judgement of his peers or by the law of the land. To no one will we sell, to no one will we deny or delay right or justice.'

These principles were exported to the United States and the American Bar Association erected this memorial in 1957. It is maintained by the Magna Carta Trust, chaired by the Master of the Rolls, one of the most important people in the English legal system.

Magna Carta Memorial.

6. Continue in the same direction to a cross path at the Kennedy Memorial. To visit the memorial, turn left and then retrace your steps.

Once through the gate you are on American soil, given to the United States in memory of the assassinated President. There is much symbolism in the design and setting, explained on a nearby board. The white structure that can be seen on top of the hill is the Air Force Memorial. This commemorates by name the over 20,000 air crew killed in World War II who have no known grave.

7. Carry on along the path then bear right at a fork to the left of two identical buildings, which houses the teashop.

The two lodges were designed by Sir Edward Lutyens and built in memory of Lord Fairhaven whose wife and sons gave the Meads to the National Trust in 1931. Cooper's Hill, which overlooks Runnymede, was given to the Trust in 1963 by Egham Urban District Council.

8. After tea, cross the road to a path by the river and follow it downstream, back to the start.

We don't know very much about what actually happened at the historic meeting between the barons and King John or where the Magna Carta was sealed; popular tradition says that it was on Magna Carta Island which the route passes. The word 'Runnymede' means 'council island meadow'. After the reluctant King John had sealed the charter, copies were distributed throughout the land. Some alterations were subsequently made and the third and final version was confirmed by Edward I in 1297.

Walk 4
VIRGINIA WATER AND
WINDSOR GREAT PARK

*W*indsor Great Park, once royal hunting grounds, is now freely open to the public and contains one of the largest stretches of ornamental water in England. This interesting walk visits the main features in the southern end of the park. Equally suitable for all times of year, the route has woodland, water, hills and glades, and there is a succession of flowering shrubs lending colour, culminating in the glorious display of autumn.

Savill Garden Restaurant looks out over one of the gardens within the park. It is housed in an exciting and unusual modern building, with floor to ceiling windows, to make the most of its situation and there is also an extensive terrace with tables outside in the summer. A wide variety of excellent cakes is served, together with other teatime goodies such as

31

Florentine biscuits and fruit pies and tarts. For lunch there is a tempting salad bar and jacket potatoes with a wide choice of fillings. There are other light savoury snacks, including sandwiches and pâté, as well as a selection of hot meals. It is open throughout the year from 10 am until 6 pm. Telephone: 01784 432326.

DISTANCE: 5 miles.
MAP: OS Explorer 160 Windsor, Weybridge & Bracknell.
STARTING POINT: Virginia Water car park (charge) (GR 981688).
HOW TO GET THERE: The directions start at Virginia Water car park on the A30, Staines to Basingstoke road, about 500 yards north-east of its junction with the A329.
ALTERNATIVE STARTING POINT: If you wish to visit the teashop at the beginning or end of your walk, start at Savill Garden, for which there is ample parking in the signed car park in Wick Lane, Englefield Green. You will then start the walk at point 8, turning right out of the teashop to begin the walk.

THE WALK

1. Leave the car park by the gate at the back and walk to the lake. Turn left to follow the path by the lake for about 300 yards. Follow the surfaced path round to the left, away from the lake, to the base of a waterfall and then follow the path back to the lakeside. Stay on the surfaced path until it eventually joins a drive.

This lovely lake, which looks so natural, was created in the 18th century by damming the Virginia River. The instigator of this project was William, 1st Duke of Cumberland and the lake was designed by Thomas Sandby, landscape gardener and deputy ranger of the park from 1746 to 1789; some of his original plans are preserved in the library at Windsor Castle. The dam was completed and the lake filled by 1753 but during a violent storm 15 years later, the dam was washed away. It was repaired and the lake had reached its present form by 1790.

It is a haven for wildfowl, both residents and migrants. Mandarin ducks are present all year round. Virginia Water is Britain's best breeding location for this exotic species, which comes originally from eastern Russia and China. It has escaped from captivity to become established as a breeding species. Other types of birds are also to be seen such as herons and kingfishers. In spring you may be lucky enough to see great crested grebe perform their elaborate courtship ritual.

The waterfall, carrying overflow from the lake, is a man-made feature. It was built using stone from Farnham, some 16 miles away. Bringing the heavy blocks here was a considerable problem because their great weight bent or broke the iron

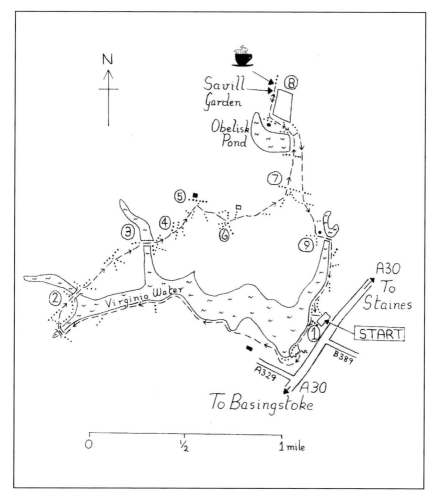

and oak axles of the carts used to carry them. Finally, green alder wood was used to make axles and this was flexible enough to bend without breaking.

The masonry columns on the left overlooking the lake come from the Temple of Serapis at Leptis Magna in Libya. They were intended for the portico of the British Museum but presented to the Prince Regent, later George IV, and eventually re-erected here as a romantic ruin. Beyond the columns, a tunnel under the A329 leads to Fort Belvedere, the home of the Duke of Windsor before he became Edward VIII in 1936.

2. Turn right and soon cross a bridge over an arm of the lake. After crossing the bridge, walk on a path to the right of, and parallel with, the drive.

3. Rejoin the drive and turn right as far as a complex path junction. Continue along the drive, signed 'Cumberland Gate 1 mile, Smiths Lawn $1/4$ mile', for 175 yards. (Do not take the path into Valley Gardens at this point.)

4. Bear right on a path into Valley Gardens. Continue ahead at the top of a rise where a path joins on the right.

There is an excellent view to the right across Valley Garden, notable for its flowering shrubs and particularly colourful in spring and autumn.

5. Some 200 yards after the top of the rise, turn right through gates on a path into the Heather Garden. (Note: if you arrive at the Guards Polo Club you have gone too far.) Follow the gravelled path through the garden to a gate.

6. Cross a drive and continue in the same direction, on a surfaced path, to a complex junction of paths and drives.

☕ **7.** Continue in the same direction on a surfaced drive signed 'Savill Garden and car park $1/2$ mile'. Pass the Obelisk Pond and obelisk to the Savill building containing the tea shop on the left.

The obelisk was raised by George II to mark the achievements of his son William, 1st Duke of Cumberland, who was appointed Ranger of Windsor Great Park after his victory over Bonnie Prince Charlie at Culloden in 1746.

Savill Garden, open all year from 10 am until 6 pm, or dusk if earlier and, for which there is a charge, was started in 1932 by Sir Eric Savill, the royal gardener. The flowering shrubs, such as rhododendrons and camellias, and herbaceous borders were laid out in 35 acres of woodland and were designed to provide colour all year round.

8. After tea, retrace your steps to the Obelisk Pond. Just after the pond starts on the right, turn left. At a T junction with a cross path after 50 yards, turn right and follow a clear path, crossing one drive then joining a second to continue in the same direction as far as the totem pole on the left.

The totem pole in Windsor Great Park.

The totem pole was a gift to the Queen to celebrate the centenary of the founding of British Columbia and was erected here in 1958. Carved from a single Western red cedar, it is a fine example of traditional Pacific Coast art, which embodies the history of tribes from Vancouver Island. The figures represent mythical ancestors and an explanatory key can be found at the base.

9. At the totem pole turn left, signed 'Wheatsheaf car park and hotel 1/2 mile'. Follow the path round to the right to walk once more beside the lake back to the start.

This walk has explored the south end of Windsor Great Park, which has been royal land since Saxon times and still belongs to the crown. It is one fragment of Windsor Forest that once extended as far as Reading and Guildford. Henry III had a small moated house near here but the site has been lost. Beneath the water is the line of a Roman road from Staines to Bath. The park is said to have its own ghost, Herne the Hunter, who only appears in times of national crisis.

Walk 5
BURNHAM BEECHES

*T*hough he knew many of the world's most notable forests, E. H. Wilson, director of Arnold Arboretum in Harvard, USA, cherished his visit to Burnham Beeches as one of the highlights of his life. An area of natural woodland, bought by the Corporation of London in 1880 as one of the capital's lungs, Burnham Beeches is a National Nature Reserve and a treasure house of wildlife interest. Though this is essentially a woodland walk, there are different habitats throughout the Beeches reflecting differences in geology and past management and this superb walk visits them all. This short walk is definitely one to savour, to take slowly with your eyes and ears open.

The Beeches Café is part of the new (autumn 2007) Visitor Centre. The opening hours vary but are at least 10 am to 4 pm every day of the year except Christmas Day, despite having no indoor accommodation. There are lots of tables outside as this is a popular spot. It offers a good range of cakes, as well as a selection of sandwiches and filled jacket potatoes. The building is designed to be environmentally friendly and, at the time of writing, has an unusual turf roof. It will be interesting to see how they get on with this in a dry year, though I am told it is growing in a generous depth of soil.

DISTANCE: 3 miles.
MAP: OS Explorer 172 Chiltern Hills East.
STARTING POINT: Park Lane car park, Burnham Beeches (GR 943856).
HOW TO GET THERE: From junction 2 of the M40 take the A355 towards Slough for about a quarter of a mile. Take the first road on the right, signed 'Taplow 6 Burnham 5 Littleworth Cmm 2' for about 1¼ miles. When the road bends right carry on in the same direction along Abbey Park Lane, signed to 'Burnham Beeches'. After about ½ mile turn left along Boveney Wood Lane and continue as it becomes Park Lane to a small car park on the left after about ½ mile.
ALTERNATIVE STARTING POINT: If you wish to visit the teashop at the beginning or end of your walk, use the main Burnham Beeches parking area at Lord Mayor's Drive. You will then start the walk at point 10.

THE WALK

Note: Burnham Beeches is freely open to those on foot. This means that there are many small, informal paths. The route described is all on major paths and drives but please follow the directions carefully, especially in autumn when fallen leaves make paths less obvious.

 1. Return to the lane and turn left for 250 yards. (Alternatively, you can easily walk inside the wood parallel with the lane though there is no specific path.)

2. Turn sharp left along Morton Drive.

In 1879 Burnham Beeches came on the market, advertised as land suitable for building 'superior residences'. A prominent naturalist, Francis George Heath, tried to enlist support for saving the area with its magnificent trees and persuaded the Corporation of the City of London to act. A new law, the Open Spaces Act of 1878, allowed the Corporation to buy unenclosed and commonland on the edge of London. However, there was a complication: there were two enclosed areas in the middle of the commonland. This was solved by the local MP, Sir Henry Peek, who bought the entire lot and then sold the unenclosed parts on to the Corporation. One

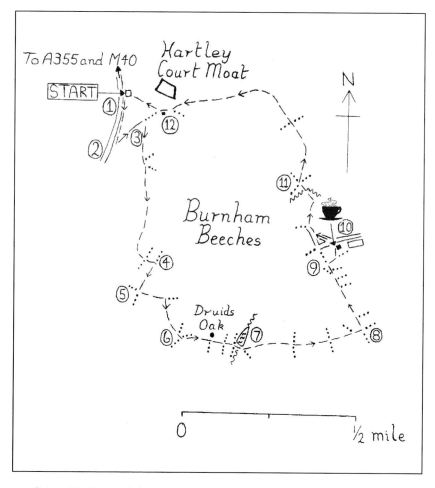

condition Sir Henry did insist upon, as part of the agreement, was that the Corporation pay for roads to be built to allow him access to the land he retained and these roads are named after people involved with the Corporation at that time. Until relatively recently, most of these were open to traffic, hence the surfacing and the speed humps. In recent years they have almost all been closed to cars and make excellent safe and easy walking.

3. Turn right along Dimsdale Drive for about 250 yards to a large wooden post. Some 10 yards after passing the post bear right to continue in the same direction and follow the path downhill for a good ¹⁄₂ mile to a cross track at the bottom of a valley.

Burnham Beeches has probably been wooded ever since the forest returned after the last Ice Age. In the past it was used as wood pasture, a dual purpose management scheme. The trees were pollarded. This means the branches were cut at head height to provide fuel and wood for small building jobs. The trees have the capacity to sprout new branches and can be cut on a 12 to 15 year rotation. Lopping them at head height keeps the succulent new growth safe from the animals which are allowed to graze the forest floor beneath. Cutting the branches in this way may seem rather brutal but it has the effect of prolonging the tree's life! A beech tree would ordinarily live for about 250 years but pollarding allows the tree to live for 400 years or more and grow into the gnarled giants for which Burnham Beeches is famous. From the middle of the 19th century onwards, the use of wood as a fuel declined as coal became more readily available. There was no longer the same need to harvest a crop from the trees and pollarding declined. It is thought that at the end of the 18th century there were about 3,000 pollards in Burnham Beeches but now the number is down to just over 500. Many of the trees have not been cut for nearly 200 years. It is very important to conserve these old trees as they are a vital habitat for many tiny animals and there are very few places that have as many ancient pollards as Burnham Beeches. Old trees are carefully repollarded to prolong their lives and a programme of cutting younger trees has started to provide the next generation of pollards. The large, unpollarded trees are relatively young in tree terms.

4. Turn right along the track for 210 yards.

5. Turn left uphill. At a fence at the top of the hill turn right alongside the fence to emerge on a surfaced drive by a gate.

6. Go through the gate, cross the drive and take a path to the right of the drive that leads to a pond. Continue ahead with the pond on your left.

To the left of this path is the most ancient tree in the Beeches, estimated to be 700 years or more old. It is fenced to help protect its roots from the damaging effect of trampling. Called the Druids Oak, there is no documented reason for this particular tree having that name; it is probably a bit of Victorian whimsy. Several named trees are marked on old maps but are no longer around. His Majesty was a huge beech pollard that had a girth of 28 feet in 1931. Sadly, it lost its crown in the severe storms of 1987, though the stump remains. Another was the Maiden Tree, said to be the only major tree in the woods that was not pollarded.
   A particularly attractive spot in summer with water lilies in bloom and colourful dragon flies darting above them, this pond and another pond upstream are not natural. They were created by the damming of a stream in about 1800 and were

used for sheep dipping until well into the 19th century. During the Second World War the Beeches were fenced off and used by the Army for exercises and maintaining vehicles. The concrete retaining walls were built then and the water in the ponds used for washing vehicles.

A family called Grote had a cottage near here and entertained many famous figures from music and literature who visited Burnham Beeches. Jenny Lind, the soprano, visited the Grotes several times whilst touring England. She used to practise arias near this pond and a plaque marks the spot. Felix Mendelssohn was another regular visitor who apparently often got lost while walking in the woods – a fate I hope you have avoided.

7. At the end of the pond bear left and follow the path ahead to a surfaced drive.

8. Turn left and walk along the drive as far as the first metal barrier, crossing a cattle grid.

9. Some 40 yards after the barrier turn right and then left to the Visitor Centre and teashop.

10. From the Visitor Centre turn left along the main drive for 30 yards then take the first drive on the right to a wooden gate across the drive. Some 15 yards after the gate, bear right off Halse Drive and follow the main path downhill, soon bearing left to a wooden footbridge, then uphill for 40 yards to a 5-way junction.

Burnham Beeches lies on gravels but the details of its geology are very complex. Where a rock more permeable to water, such as chalk, meets less permeable clay, for example, streams can suddenly disappear at a swilly hole, a corruption of swallow hole. There is a line of swilly holes along this small valley, surface evidence of changes in the underlying geology.

11. Take the left-hand of two paths on the right to a drive at a junction. Continue ahead along McAuliffe Drive, following it round as it swings left, to a junction of drives and a wooden shelter.

One of the most obvious little animals is the wood ant, which lives in huge nests with extensive underground sections. There are several good examples of big nests by the drive.

To the right of the drive, marked by a plaque, are the remains of a moated homestead dating to sometime between the 12th and 14th centuries. It is variously

A pollarded beech.

called Hartley Court, Harlequin's and Hardicanute's Moat. *The moat itself, often containing water in the winter, is the most obvious feature. It encloses a rectangular area of about 1½ acres, with evidence of a house on the north side and a well. There is also an outer ditch and bank enclosing the moat and a larger area of about 9 acres. There was probably a fence on the bank and its purpose was to protect the cultivated land from deer and pigs grazing in the surrounding woods.*

12. Turn right then fork right after 30 yards and follow the path back to the start.

Walk 6
DOWNLEY COMMON AND HUGHENDEN VALLEY

Benjamin Disraeli knew and loved the Chilterns, making his home at Hughenden, just outside High Wycombe. This easy walk visits his home for tea and much of the route, especially on the return leg, is through beautiful beechwoods, for which the Chilterns are justifiably famous. There is little climbing but nonetheless there are some excellent views to be enjoyed.

 The Stable Tea Rooms at Hughenden Manor provide the usual excellent National Trust fare. As well as cakes, a High Tea with sandwiches and scones and a Cream Tea with clotted cream are served. An alternative is toast with jam made from fruit grown on the Hughenden Estate. Light lunches of crusty rolls with a good choice of tasty fillings are available until 1.45 pm and soup is served in the colder months. They are open Wednesday to Sunday and Bank Holiday Mondays from the end of March until the end of October, between 11 am until 5 pm. The Stable is also open weekends in March, November and the first half of December to 4 pm. Telephone: 01494 755576.

When the tea rooms are closed, food is available at the Le De Spencer Arms, passed early in the walk.

DISTANCE: 3 miles.

MAP: OS Explorer 172 Chiltern Hills East.

STARTING POINT: Downley Common (GR 848957).

HOW TO GET THERE: From the A40 on the outskirts of High Wycombe towards West Wycombe at traffic lights, take a minor road, Plomer Hill, signed 'Downley 1'. Follow this through Downley and continue when it is signed as a 'No Through Road'. There is a small parking area on the left just after a sharp right-hand bend. If this is full, there are several other spots round the common where a car can be left without causing inconvenience.

ALTERNATIVE STARTING POINT: If you wish to visit the teashop at the beginning or end of your walk, start at Hughenden Manor where there is a car park for visitors. Access is from the A4128 north of High Wycombe. You will then start the walk at point 6.

THE WALK

Downley started as a typical Chiltern village that has become joined to High Wycombe by the growth of the town. It works hard to maintain a separate identity and has its own Parish Council.

1. Continue along the road until it ends at a T junction with a track. Turn left and fork left after 40 yards, soon passing the Le De Spencer Arms. Continue past some metal bollards into a beechwood.

2. Some 60 yards after the bollards, bear right off the main path on a much smaller path marked with occasional white blobs on trees. After 100 yards cross a path marked by a signpost. After a further 75 yards bear left at a less than obvious fork and continue ahead to a lane, ignoring all paths to the left.

There are some fine beech trees in this area. Beech is a lovely tree with smooth, grey bark and glossy green leaves. It is especially beautiful in the spring, when the newly emerged leaves are so fresh, and in the autumn when they change from gold to orange to brown. Southern England is the northernmost extent of the beech's range. Some individual beech trees are found further north but no extensive beechwoods. The fruit of the beech is a three sided nut, sometimes called mast, enclosed in a

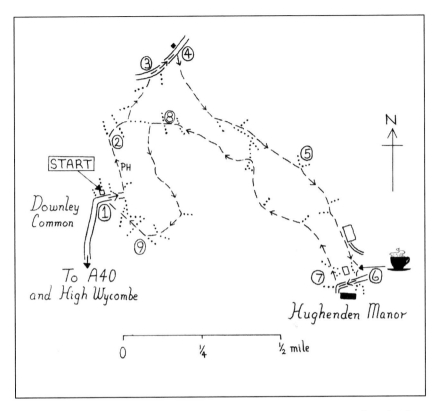

capsule with quite soft prickles on the outside. Fruit in quantity is produced only in irregular so-called mast years, sometimes at quite long intervals. In other years a late spring frost interferes with the setting of the nuts or a cool summer prevents their ripening. Beech has such a dense canopy that it absorbs a lot of the light and not much can grow underneath it so the forest beneath beech is very open.

3. Turn right for about 200 yards.

4. Opposite Oakswood House, turn right onto a fenced and hedged path that ends at a metal kissing gate into a field. Continue in the same direction along the right-hand side of the first field and across a second to a kissing gate onto a track.

5. Turn right. Follow the track into and through a wood and carry on in the same direction, past a car park, along a surfaced drive to the tea rooms down some steps on the left.

45

6. Leave the stable yard with the tea rooms through a gated arch and go ahead to a T junction in front of Hughenden Manor. Turn right.

Disraeli spent his youth at Bradenham Manor, which lies between West Wycombe and Princes Risborough. He stood as MP for Wycombe but was defeated. Five years later he was elected as Member for Maidstone and the citizens of Wycombe overcame their objections and subscribed to illuminations in his honour! He bought Hughenden in 1848 for £35,000 and shared it with his wife, Mary Ann, for thirty-three years. When she died he was inconsolable and the Hughenden paper afterwards had a black border. It passed to the National Trust in 1946 and contains much of Disraeli's furniture, books and other memorabilia. The park in which it stands is shared with Wycombe District Council. The house is open to the public on Wednesday to Saturday and Bank Holiday Mondays from 2 pm till 6 pm between April and October and at weekends in March. Telephone: 01494 532580.

Disraeli is buried in the churchyard by the east wall of St Michael and All Angels just down the hill from the manor. The church has been here since 1145 but not much remains of the old structure. It was extensively restored in 1874/75. It has a fine series of tombs, which are curiosities because they are forgeries carried out by a local family, the Wellesbournes, in Tudor times to try and establish a connection with the great family of de Montfort.

7. When the surfaced drive bends left, turn right on a woodland path which contours round the hillside, rising slightly to begin with. Ignore all side turns and stick with the occasional purple waymark to eventually reach a cross track signed 'Naphill' to the right..

8. Cross the track to take a path opposite, leaving the purple waymarking. The path initially climbs steeply and is marked by white arrows on trees. At the top of the hill turn left and follow the path just inside the wood, passing to the left of a deep pit. Ignore all paths on the left and follow the path round to the right. Continue past a gated path to the right as you cross a ditch to an oblique T-junction with a cross path.

9. Turn right uphill out of the wood. Just before some wooden posts marking a track, bear half left across the common and by a cricket pitch, back to the start.

Walk 7
WEST WYCOMBE

West Wycombe is a Chiltern village of outstanding architectural interest with a manor house open to the public. This fairly energetic circuit makes its way there across the hills, including a fine section along a ridge, and so involves some climbing but the effort is amply rewarded by some excellent views. The route also passes through an important nature reserve so there is much of interest to see on the way and plenty of time needs to be allowed to get the best from this highly recommended walk.

West Wycombe Garden Centre is located in a walled garden dating back to at least 1754. The Old Gardener's Cottage Teashop has a small but attractive interior and several tables outside protected by a pergola with views of the Chiltern Hills crossed in this walk. Open every day throughout the year between 10 am (10.30 am on Sundays) until 5 pm, they serve a good selection of cakes, scones and other teatime goodies, including the

Gardener's cream tea. For a light lunch there are snacks such as ploughman's or sandwiches and quiche served with salad. Tempting on a cold day is hot chocolate served with whipped cream and marshmallows. Telephone: 01494 438635.

DISTANCE: 4½ miles.

MAP: OS Explorer 172 Chiltern Hills East.

STARTING POINT: Old Oxford Road near Piddington, where there is plenty of space to park without causing inconvenience to other road users (GR 814941).

HOW TO GET THERE: On the A40 between High Wycombe and Stokenchurch, about a mile west of West Wycombe, there is a section of over ½ mile where the old road, parallel with the modern road, has been maintained. It is signed 'Piddington' at the east (West Wycombe) end. The walk starts about 200 yards from the east end at the first road connection to the A40.

ALTERNATIVE STARTING POINT: If you wish to visit the teashop at the beginning or end of your walk, start in West Wycombe where there is ample parking in the car park next to the garden centre. The teashop is in the garden centre. You will then start the walk at point 7.

THE WALK

1. Cross the A40 and take a public bridleway along a hedged track up the hillside. Bear left to continue in the same direction at the first fork, just inside a wood, and right at a second fork at the top of the hill. Ignore all side turns and follow the main track down to a lane.

2. Cross the lane to a path slightly left to continue in more or less the same direction, crossing two further lanes.

3. Follow the path up the other side of the valley, initially walking with a hedge on the right and then following the main path slightly left uphill. Near the top go through a small gate into mature woodland and continue uphill to emerge in a small clearing at the top.

The Chilterns are made of chalk, laid down millions of years ago at the bottom of the sea, and pushed up into hills in the same earth movements that formed the Alps and the South Downs. Left to themselves the hills would be covered in oak and beechwoods but large areas have been grazed for hundreds of years, which has encouraged the development of short turf rich in flowers. In more recent decades sheep farming in the old way has been less profitable and even grazing by rabbits

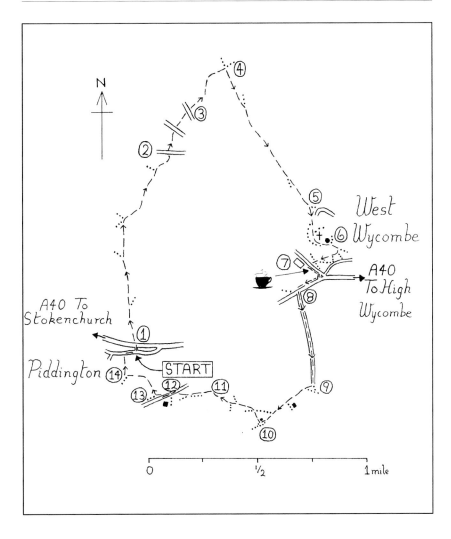

declined as their population was decimated by myxomatosis. This allowed the chalk grassland to be invaded by coarser grasses and shrubs such as dogwood and hawthorn have become established, as has happened here. Attempts are made to conserve the grass by controlled grazing and clearing the scrub by hand. This hillside faces south and can get very hot, as you will notice if you do this walk on a sunny day in summer. These conditions are ideal for invertebrates – creepy crawlies. Some 26 species of butterfly are recorded regularly and 108 species of spider have been identified.

4. Turn right. When a path joins from the left continue along the ridge for about ½ mile to an open area used as a car park.

5. Leave the main path and head to the right of the tower with a golden ball on top, St Lawrence's church. Pass the church on your left then follow the path by the wall on the left round to a flint structure, the mausoleum.

St Lawrence's church is built in the ditch and bank of an Iron Age hill fort and is an ancient foundation. It was originally the parish church of the lost village of Haveringdon, once a little way back along the ridge and abandoned in the late 18th century, probably due to lack of water. Only the ruined chancel and part of the tower remained when Sir Francis Dashwood, the second baronet, turned his attention to it. The nave is like a classical drawing room with stalls and lectern with comfortable rosewood armchairs, exquisite paintings, stucco decorations on the ceiling and walls and a marble floor. Some brasses and monuments from the original church were preserved. The most unusual feature of all is the golden ball on top of the tower. It holds ten or twelve people and is reached by a ladder on the outside. John Wilkes, a friend of Dashwood, described it as 'the best Globe tavern I was ever in'. It is possible to visit the church tower on weekday afternoons in summer and a small charge is made.

The fortifications that defended the Iron Age village can be seen running parallel with the churchyard fence and at the eastern end are cut by the mausoleum. This is a large open hexagon of flint with Portland stone dressing, which contains memorials to members of the Dashwood family and their friends. For example, in the centre is an urn on a pedestal commemorating Francis Dashwood's wife who died in 1769.

6. From the mausoleum follow the obvious path downhill towards High Wycombe. After 100 yards turn right down some steps and continue across the hillside in the same direction when the steps end, to a road. West Wycombe Garden Centre with its teashop is across the road.

High Wycombe, once known as Chipping Wycombe, is a very old settlement, being situated on one of the few rivers in the Chilterns – the Wye. There are many traces of pre-Roman and Roman occupation and the age of the parish church of All Saints is indicated by its consecration by Wulfstan who was Bishop of Worcester from 1062 to 1095. The key to the town's development is to be found growing all over the surrounding hills – the beechwoods – for they and the men who worked them led to High Wycombe becoming a leading centre of the furniture industry. It is still an important part of the town's economy. The town centre has received attention from the developers though the High Street retains some of its Georgian character. Sadly, charmless housing estates have crept over its surrounding hills, forever spoiling the beauty of its setting.

7. Return to the road and turn right to a junction with the main road, the A40. To explore West Wycombe turn left and the entrance to West Wycombe Park is across the road. To continue with the route turn right for 200 yards.

For more than 250 years West Wycombe has been associated with the Dashwood family. West Wycombe village was bought from Sir John Dashwood in 1929 and given to the National Trust five years later so that it could be preserved as a living example of an English village. Only two new houses have been built in this century and there are examples of many types of English architecture from the 16th century onwards. It is well worth taking the time to explore in detail. The National Trust produces an architectural trail guide round the village that can be bought from the village shop opposite the George and Dragon.

West Wycombe House and Park were given to the National Trust in 1943. The house was rebuilt in the late 1700s by the second baronet, now best remembered for the Hellfire Club. He was a much travelled and cultivated man who was interested in classical architecture and had the house rebuilt in the Palladian style, dammed the infant river Wye to form a lake and employed Humphrey Repton to lay out the grounds. The house is open to the public in June, July and August, Sunday to Thursday, from 2 pm until 5 pm. The grounds only are also open in April and May on Wednesday and Sunday during the same hours. Telephone: 01494 524411.

The 18th-century Sir Francis Dashwood succeeded to his father's estate and fortune when he was sixteen. He was a man of considerable energy, wealth and achievement, not to say profligacy. He was Chancellor of the Exchequer (said at the time to be the worst ever) and Postmaster General. He rewrote the Book of Common Prayer into everyday English and built the straight road into High Wycombe you can see from the top of the hill. Today his popular reputation is solely concerned with the Hellfire Club, supposedly founded for the practice of black magic, first at Medmenham Abbey and then in the caves behind the village. The name the group gave themselves was the Brotherhood of St Francis or Dashwood's Apostles and half of Dashwood's Cabinet colleagues were members. They were undoubtedly up to no good but wild parties are more likely than devil worship.

The caves behind the village are not natural. They were dug to provide raw materials for the new road to High Wycombe that Dashwood built to relieve local poverty and unemployment. They go back into the hillside for about ¼ mile and are cleaned out, lit and provided with displays supposed to recreate times past. They are

The mausoleum on West Wycombe Hill.

open every day between 11 am and 5 pm in the summer from March to October and at weekends all year.

8. Turn left along a tiny, dead end road, Toweridge Lane, which climbs up to and through woods and has a good view of West Wycombe House on the left.

9. Immediately after the tarmac surface ends, turn right on a public bridleway along a track. When the gravel track bends left to some barns, continue in the same direction. At a fork take the right branch.

10. Immediately after a telecommunications aerial on the right, turn right on a small and poorly signed path: there is the usual white arrow near the bottom of a small tree. This is not at all obvious: if you rejoin the other branch of the track, you have missed it! The path soon leads into a field where it is not always visible on the ground, and heads straight across and into a wood where it becomes a more obvious track. Follow the main track round to the left and as it more or less contours along the hillside to the edge of the wood.

11. Immediately on leaving the wood go through a gap on the right into a field then turn left to walk with a hedge on the left. Continue in the same direction when the hedge ends to a stile on the right giving into a strip of woodland. The path soon leads to a lane.

12. Turn left, passing the entrance to Bullock's Farm, to a track on the right. Take this track for 50 yards to a stile on the right.

13. Cross the stile and follow a sometimes faint path through woodland, initially mature trees and then a recently replanted area. This eventually leads to a stile into a field.

14. Cross the stile and turn right down the field to a stile by a gate. Turn right, back to the start.

Walk 8
MARLOW AND TEMPLE LOCK

*M*arlow *is a most attractive Thames-side town with its front door on the river and its back door onto the Chilterns. It has a long history, many fine buildings and a remarkable number of literary associations for such a small town. This varied route starts near the river in Marlow and passes some of the most interesting parts of the town before leaving the bustle behind for the quiet of some outstanding Chiltern woodland. The path then drops down to the banks of the Thames where an easy stroll by the river leads back to Marlow.*

At weekends and in the summer, teas are served in the garden of the lock keeper's cottage at Temple Lock, beautifully situated on an island. This is just the place to idle away an hour on a sunny afternoon, overlooking a lovely stretch of the river with the traffic through the lock to watch. A small selection of delicious cakes is available with cookies or ice cream as alternatives. The opening hours are flexible, depending rather on the weather since there is no indoor accommodation, but teas are generally served from 11 am until 5.30 pm on summer weekends and later in the school holidays. Telephone: 01628 824333.

When tea is not being served at Temple Lock, there are many alternatives in Marlow. See also walk 9.

DISTANCE: 6 miles.
MAP: OS Explorer 172 Chiltern Hills East.
STARTING POINT: Pound Lane car park, Marlow (charge) (GR 848862).
HOW TO GET THERE: Directions are given from the car park in Pound Lane, Marlow. This is just off the High Street, a couple of hundred yards on the town side of Marlow Bridge.
ALTERNATIVE STARTING POINT: There is no vehicular access for the public to Temple Lock so it is not possible to start this walk from there.

THE WALK

1. From the entrance to the car park turn left along Pound Lane for 20 yards then turn right on a path between high walls. Alternatively, to see more of Marlow, turn right along Pound Lane then left up the High Street to the far end.

Many of the buildings on the High Street are Georgian behind their modern shop fronts. The building facing down the High Street, now the Crown, was once the Town Hall. The obelisk outside shows the distance to local places of importance, such as High Wycombe and Oxford, and Hatfield some 36 miles away in the next county! The reason for this anomaly is that the rich and powerful Cecil family caused the Reading and Hatfield Turnpike Trust to improve the road to shorten the bumping, agonising journey of the Cecils, martyrs to gout, from their estate at Hatfield to the Bath road at Reading. It became known as the Gout Track.

2. Turn left along West Street and continue for about ¹/₂ mile until opposite the far end of Pound Lane.

West Street has attracted a remarkable number of literati. Shelley lived at number 104. After his first wife drowned herself, he married his mistress, Mary, and it was while living in Marlow that she finished 'Frankenstein'. Shelley was introduced to Marlow by another poet, Thomas Love Peacock, who also lived in West Street, at number 47. In more modern times a most prolific writer, G.P.R. James, lived further along West Street. He is almost entirely forgotten today but in the middle of the 19th century was very popular and friends with all the great literary figures of the age. Towards the end of the First World War T.S. Eliot moved to Marlow with his wife to

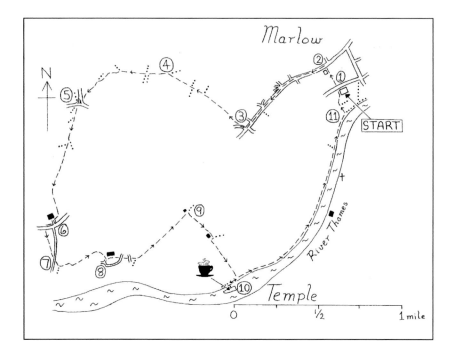

escape the bombing and they lived at 31 West Street. He travelled to London every day by cycling to Maidenhead to catch the train.

Marlow's most famous son today is a giant in a different field. Steve Redgrave has won five gold medals for rowing and started his career at Great Marlow School.

3. Turn right along Henley Road signed as a public footpath. After 80 yards bear right on a signed path and follow this along a dry valley, eventually climbing to a T-junction with a fenced path.

4. Turn left. At a cross path continue into a wood then, after about 300 yards, turn left on a waymarked path. Go ahead when a path joins on the right then follow the waymarks as the path turns left. Follow this path through to a lane, emerging near a fork.

In this part of the Chilterns, chalk is overlaid with later deposits of gravel, brickearth and clay with flints. The brickearth was extracted in the past and the pits can still be seen. Part of the woods is Marlow Common. Contrary to what many people suppose, common land is not owned by the public. It means someone other than the owner has rights over the land; in this case the right to remove timber for house building and repair, known as lessor housebote.

5. Cross over to the far branch and turn left. Cross another lane then follow a broad path ahead. Look for a low earth bank on the right. Stay on the path with the bank on the right, bearing right at a fork. Soon after this the path crosses the bank and continues with it on your left. Stay on this path through the wood to a main road, crossing the bank a second time and then walking by Danesfield School.

Earth banks are commonly seen in woodlands. They were used to define boundaries. This one probably dates back to at least Saxon times and still forms the boundary between Medmenham and Great Marlow parishes.

6. Turn right on a path on the road verge that leads to a signed public footpath across the road. Follow the path, rather faint at the time of writing, to a metal kissing gate onto a surfaced drive.

7. Take a path opposite down to high double gates. Turn left in front of the gates and follow the path through the wood and then round a golf course. This eventually becomes a track that leads to Harleyford Golf Club buildings.

A variety of recreational facilities have been developed on the Harleyford estate, including a golf course, caravan site and marina. Harleyford Manor was built in 1755 for Sir William Clayton, a substantial landowner in this part of the Chilterns.

8. A few yards after the track is surfaced it bends right. Go ahead on a surfaced path and follow the path between buildings, across a drive and down through woodland into a timber yard and on across a drive. Bear round to the left to a kissing gate beside a field gate. Follow a faint path close to a fence on the left to a track by a house.

9. Turn right on a surfaced drive to a farm, taking the path to the left past the house then returning to the drive. Continue on the drive to the river, ignoring a track on the left. Turn right to Temple Lock and the teashop.

Temple Lock was originally built in 1773 to replace the original flash lock (see walk 13). There used to be a ferry here but it stopped operating in the 1950s. Since 1989

The Thames at Bisham.

walkers have again been able to cross from Buckinghamshire to Berkshire, using the award winning Temple footbridge about 200 yards upriver from the lock.

10. After tea, recross the lock and turn right along the path on the river bank. Follow this back to Marlow.

Across the river is Bisham Abbey. Today it is owned by the Sports Council who use it as a national sports centre and a wide variety of sports at a high level are coached here. It is often used as a headquarters by the England football team.

The present building is mainly Tudor and was built by Henry VIII for his fourth wife, Anne of Cleves. For many years it belonged to the Hoby family and they were custodians of Elizabeth I for three years while Mary was on the throne. The building is said to be haunted by the ghost of one Lady Hoby. She punished her little boy for blotting his copy book by locking him in a cupboard. Later that day she was called away to another part of the country and it was some time before she returned home. She had forgotten to release her son or tell anyone where he was and he had starved to death in the cupboard. She is supposed to roam the building, wailing and wringing her hands in remorse. It is said that some blotted 16th century copybooks were discovered during renovation work...

11. As you approach Marlow, take a surfaced path on the left through the park, back to the start.

Walk 9
MARLOW AND WINTER HILL

This walk is unusual for this book because the more energetic and longer section comes after tea – so make sure you are well fuelled up! The reason for this break with my usual custom is that the views are much better if you do the walk clockwise. The route starts on the banks of the Thames between Bourne End and Marlow and approaches Marlow along the river, passing a pub where Jerome K. Jerome wrote part of Three Men in a Boat. *He described Marlow as a 'bustling, lively little town' where 'the river itself is at its best'. All that is as true today as when it was first written. We then cross the river at the famous suspension bridge to climb steeply onto Winter Hill with its extensive views before a gentle descent to Bourne End to recross the river and return to the start.*

 Burgers is a traditional tearoom behind a Swiss patisserie. It has been a family-run business since 1942 when Eric and Marie Burger brought a touch

59

of Switzerland to Buckinghamshire six years after arriving in England. The cakes are outstanding and with a very few exceptions everything is made on the premises. Cream teas comprise Yorkshire blend tea, scones with preserve and cream, and a cake. For lunch there is soup, sandwiches, various specials or an exceptional Welsh rarebit made to their own recipe. The tearoom is behind the shop and you will find it hard to resist the exquisite chocolates. At Christmas they sell wonderful Christmas cakes and puddings and at Easter they have their famous chocolate eggs. Burgers is on the High Street at the junction with Station Road and is open every day except Sunday until 5.30 pm. Telephone: 01628 483389.

If you choose to do this walk on a Sunday there are several other places of refreshment in Marlow on or near the High Street.

DISTANCE: 6 miles.
MAP: OS Explorer 172 Chiltern Hills East.
STARTING POINT: Spade Oak car park between Marlow and Bourne End (GR 884875).
HOW TO GET THERE: From the A4155, Marlow Bourne End road, at Well End 1½ miles east of its junction with the A404 Marlow by-pass, take a minor road, Coldmoorholme Lane, signed 'Spade Oak ½', to a car park on the right.
ALTERNATIVE STARTING POINT: If you wish to visit the teashop at the beginning or end of your walk, start in Marlow where there is ample parking in public car parks in Pound Lane and West Street, both of which have charges. The teashop is on the High Street at the junction with Station Road. You will then start the walk at point 4.

THE WALK

1. Turn right out of the car park along a lane. Go across the railway to the river bank and turn right to walk upstream. Continue beside the river under the bypass. Just after the path becomes surfaced follow the main path as it bears right away from the river to a road.

2. Turn left.

☕ **3.** Some 40 yards after Thamesfield Gardens on the right turn left along a walled footpath to a road with the river rushing past at the end. Turn right for 20 yards then left along the signed Thames Path through the churchyard onto Marlow High Street. Turn right to the teashop on the right.

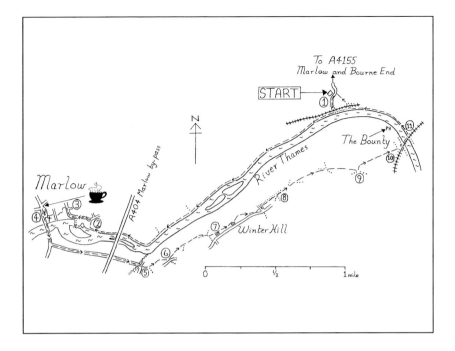

The attractive road with the river at the end led to the original wooden bridge across the Thames. This was replaced by the suspension bridge. On the river at this point and on the opposite side there were once busy wharves: Marlow was an important port sending Chiltern timber, lace and other products to London. The street was originally known as Duck Lane because it also led to the ducking stool used to reprimand the town scolds. It is now called St Peter Street after the Catholic church. This contains a relic that is supposed to be the mummified hand of St James the Apostle. In the pub by the path, the Two Brewers, Jerome K. Jerome wrote some of 'Three Men in a Boat'. See Walk 8 for more about Marlow High Street.

4. Turn left out of the teashop and follow the road over Marlow Bridge. Take the first road on the left, Quarry Wood Road, signed 'Cookham Dean 1¼', for about half a mile, going under the bypass.

There has been a bridge at Marlow for at least 600 years. The present structure was built in the 1830s, about the same time the church was rebuilt and the two together make a fine vista. It is a suspension bridge with a span of 225 feet designed by W. Tierney Clark whose greatest monument is the bridge across the Danube connecting Buda and Pest. Marlow Bridge is a scaled-down version of the former Hammersmith Bridge, also designed by Tierney Clark. The stone towers are classical archways with slender, elegant suspension chains. These were originally made of iron, which were replaced by steel when the bridge underwent substantial renovation work in 1965.

5. When the road bends right just after a bridge across a stream, go ahead on a path that climbs through woodland to a road.

This bridge was known as the Parole Bridge. During the Napoleonic Wars prisoners held in Marlow were allowed out within one mile of the gaol and were on parole not to cross this bridge into the woods. These woods were badly affected by the great storm in 1987. As you climb through the woods, notice how young all the trees are and the remains of the fallen trees on the ground. These are slowly rotting away, and provide important habitats for the wildlife involved in this process. It is said that it takes a tree as long to rot as it takes to grow so they will be here for a long time yet.

6. Do not go onto the road but take a path on the left. After a while, the trees on the left thin and you start to get views across the river. The path eventually reaches a drive. Walk along the drive for 18 yards then bear left on a way-marked path to shortly emerge on a lane by a parking area.

This is Winter Hill, famous for its views. The expanses of water on the other side of the river are flooded gravel pits.

7. Press on in the same direction beside the lane. At the end of the second parking area, the path goes away from the lane but soon returns to it. Now watch for an unsigned path on the left. Take this and very soon cross two parallel lanes. Continue on the path (not the parallel private drive to the left of the path, Spade Oak Reach) to join a track coming in from the right.

If you miss the unsigned path and come to two tiny lanes together on the left, not to worry. Turn left on Stonehouse Lane for 30 yards then right on the path.

8. Carry on in the same direction along this track, soon crossing a stile by a metal gate. Ignore a path on the left after 35 yards and one on the right after a further 100 yards. The track leads gently downhill with excellent views left and ahead. At the bottom of the hill,

The Bounty seen from across the river.

continue with the slope on your right as far as a path on the right and a wooden walkway on the left.

9. Turn left along the walkway. When this ends, bear half right on a faint path heading across the marsh to a stile by a metal gate.

This is Cock Marsh. The flat, marshy meadow was formed by silt being deposited at the base of the slope and gradually altering the course of the river. It has been grazed by cattle since at least the Iron Age and has never been ploughed or 'improved'. This means it is an important example of an increasingly rare habitat and has been designated a Site of Special Scientific Interest. Local people bought it in 1934 for £2,800 raised by public subscription and handed it over to the National Trust. There are five prehistoric burial mounds on the 132 acres, only one of which can be clearly seen. They were excavated in 1874 and one was found to have been resused for the burial of a Saxon warrior.

The Bounty, an attractive pub overlooking the river, is the fourth building from the right and there is a stile giving access from the rear. Where the Bounty stands today there was a 30-bedroomed hotel until 1938 when it burned down. It is said that among its guests were Edward and Mrs Simpson. They are supposed to have arrived by plane, landing on the marsh behind.

10. Go under the railway and turn left to the river. Turn left and go under the railway again to find some steps on the left up to a bridge beside the railway over the river.

11. Over the bridge turn left, signed 'Thames Path Marlow 3m'. Follow the path through Bourne End Marina. Take a signed path on the right soon after Upper Thames Yacht Club over the railway to a track. Turn left along the track to a lane. Turn left back to the start.

Walk 10
REMENHAM AND
HENLEY-ON-THAMES

The outward leg of this route is quite energetic as it climbs round the side of Remenham Hill but your efforts are well rewarded by some excellent views across the Thames to the Chilterns beyond. After visiting Henley for tea, the return leg is a much easier stroll by the river beside the world famous regatta course. This circuit is highly recommended at all times of year but is particularly suitable as a winter walk (unless the river is in flood) as much of the route is on well-made tracks and lanes and so you are unlikely to encounter much mud. The one period when the walk is unsuitable is the first week in July when the river bank by the regatta course is crowded with hospitality tents.

Henley Tea Rooms has a pleasant traditional interior with friendly and efficient service and a couple of tables outside looking out to the river across the road. They offer a variety of set teas, including a cream tea with clotted cream or a cottage tea, which is malt loaf served with butter and jam and a slice of cake. There is a good choice of cakes, including a tasty carrot cake. For lunch the extensive menu ranges from sandwiches through filled jacket potatoes and salads to full meals. They are open from 9.30 am until 5.30 pm during the week and 6.30 pm at the weekend. Telephone: 01491 411412.

DISTANCE: 4 miles.
MAP: OS Explorer 172 Chiltern Hills East.
STARTING POINT: Remenham church (GR 770841).
HOW TO GET THERE: From the A4130 between Henley-on-Thames and Maidenhead, about 300 yards on the Maidenhead side of Henley Bridge, take a small road called Remenham Lane. Follow this to Remenham village where there are several parking spots by the church.
ALTERNATIVE STARTING POINT: If you wish to visit the teashop at the beginning or end of your walk, start in Henley-on-Thames where there is ample parking in the long stay car park by the station. Turn right to the river and follow the road to the teashop on the left. You will then start the walk at point 9.

THE WALK

Remenham today is a few cottages clustering round a relatively modern church, dating back to 1870. This conceals its long history, probably going back to Roman times, and the village is mentioned in the Domesday Book and the Charters of Westminster Abbey, dated 1075. The church has a recorded history of more than 1,000 years and rests on Saxon and Norman foundations. The entire population was wiped out in an outbreak of plague in the 17th century and the village never recovered from this disaster.

1. With your back to the gate into Remenham churchyard, turn left to walk with the churchyard wall on your left. After about 100 yards bear right uphill on a lane signed 'Maidenhead'.

The view from here is outstanding with Temple Island in the Thames below. This has a white 'temple' built in 1771 as a vista for Fawley Court and is the start of the regatta course. Across the river are the Chilterns, a range of low chalk hills often crowned with superb beechwoods.

2. Soon after the lane levels out cross a substantial wooden stile on

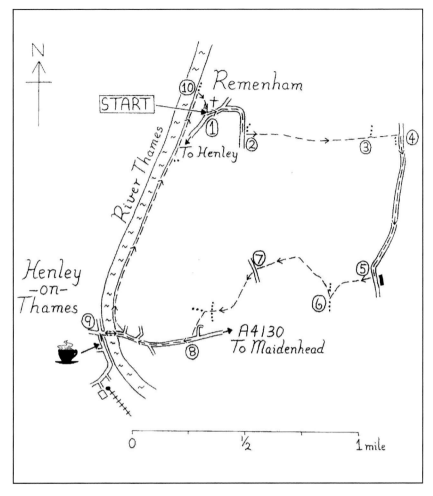

the left, next to wide metal field gates, to follow a signed path along a track across a field.

3. When the track bends left continue straight ahead on a signed path and follow this to a lane.

4. Turn right for about ½ mile.

5. When houses start on the left, turn right on a fenced public footpath.

6. At a T junction turn right on a path to the left of the drive to Common Barn. When the path emerges from woods into a field through a gate, bear half left to a stile and on across a second field to a lane.

7. Turn left for 20 yards then take a signed path over a stile on the right. Follow this through woodland. Some 30 yards after crossing a track, bear left at a fork and follow the path down to a road.

8. Turn right down into Henley. Across the bridge over the river Thames turn left to the teashop on the right.

Some sort of bridge has existed in Henley for a very long time. In the 16th century it is known to have been a wooden structure with a chapel dedicated to St Anne on the bridge itself. It was destroyed in 1642 by either Parliamentary or Royalist forces and not repaired until 1670. Whether or not the repairs were adequate, it was declared dangerous in 1754 and swept away in a great flood in 1774 and was not rebuilt until 1786. There are two carved heads on the keystones: that facing upstream represents Isis and Father Thames looks downstream.

Henley is a very interesting town to explore. On the Thames and the road to London, it was an important riverside port trading in timber, corn and malt. In the 18th century the town became a coaching stop between London and Oxford and there was much rebuilding and refronting of houses at this period. The railway arrived in 1857 and there has been further expansion since. Henley has over 300 listed buildings of many styles and periods. The Kenton Theatre in New Street was built in 1805 and is one of the oldest theatres in the country still in use. The Bull Inn in Bell Street dates in part from 1326.

9. Turn left out of the teashop back to the bridge. Recross the bridge and take a signed path on the left. After a few yards bear left to the river bank then follow the path on the bank for about a mile. As you approach Remenham the view of Temple Island with the Chilterns behind is particularly fine.

The stretch of river you are now walking beside is the famous regatta course. Henley Royal Regatta is a great rowing festival, and social occasion, which has made the town famous throughout the world. It had its origin in the first University Boat Race in June 1829. The people of Henley realised that they had one of the finest stretches of river for racing in the world, so in 1839 a public meeting was held in the Town Hall, attended by the local landed gentry and prominent townspeople. It was decided to establish a regatta with the aims of 'producing most beneficial effects to the town' and being 'a source of amusement and gratification to the neighbourhood.' The first regatta took place on 14th June 1839 with four races being held between 4 pm and 7 pm. It has now grown to five days of racing held in the first week of July with more than 350 entries from all over the world, with tents and marquees all along this stretch of river bank. The Royal part of its title originated in 1861 when Prince Albert became its patron.

10. When you see buildings on the right, watch for a signed path on the right and follow this back to Remenham church and the start.

The regatta course on the Thames.

Walk 11
HARPSDEN AND MARSH LOCK

This short walk starts at Shiplake station and climbs gently to Harpsden with its beautiful backdrop of outstanding beech woods, some of which are explored on this route. There is much of interest to see in the tiny hamlet before dropping down to the teashop and the river for a short stretch along the river bank to Marsh Lock and back to the start. Always enjoyable, this circuit is particularly suitable as a pipe opener in winter as much of the way is on tracks and lanes and the paths used are good.

 The River and Rowing Museum on the outskirts of Henley-on-Thames is housed in a modern, purpose-built structure. The Terrace Café may be accessed without visiting the museum. It is a light and airy space with floor to ceiling windows and giving onto an extensive wooden terrace with plenty of tables. Blinds at the windows are printed with river-related extracts to give you something to read with your refreshment. They serve delicious cakes, including gluten free ones. For lunch there is a choice of filled baguettes, salads and full meals. The café and museum are open every day throughout the year between 10 am and 5.30 pm, closing half an hour earlier between September and April. Telephone: 01491 415600.

DISTANCE: 5 miles.
MAP: OS Explorer 171 Chiltern Hills West.
STARTING POINT: Shiplake Station car park. (GR 776797).
HOW TO GET THERE: In Lower Shiplake on the A4155, Henley-on-Thames to Caversham road, about two miles south of Henley, turn along Station Road. Follow this to the station car park on the right.
ALTERNATIVE STARTING POINT: If you wish to visit the tea shop at the beginning or end of your walk, start at the public car park in Henley accessed past the station (charge). You will then start the walk at point 10.

THE WALK

1. Turn left out of the station car park for 75 yards to a 5-way junction. Bear half right along Northfield Avenue. At the end of the road continue in the same direction on a fenced path to a main road.

2. Cross the road and continue on a track to a lane.

3. Turn right for about ¼ mile.

4. Bear right on a signed bridleway into Harpsden and Peveril Woods. Stay on the path by a fence to emerge on a lane at a road junction.

5. Turn right for about 300 yards through Harpsden and passing St Margaret's church.

There have been people living in this dry, wooded valley ('den' or 'dene' means valley) at least since Roman times. A villa, excavated in 1909, was occupied at least until the 4th century: some of the finds are kept in Henley library and Reading Museum and there are some Roman floor tiles in the church porch. It was, and remains, a scattered community with no central village. In the Domesday book it is recorded as having 12 peasant farmers and two smallholders with an overall taxable value of £6. The ancient church has served this community for at least 800 years The present church building was probably erected in the 12th century and is worth a look, with an informative guide book available within.

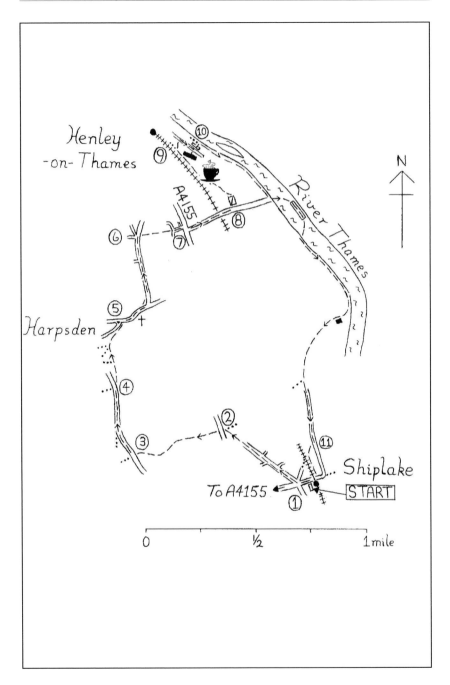

A fascinating map of Harpsden in the 16th century survives. It was made in 1586 by John Blagrave of Reading for Humphrey Forster of Harpsden Manor and is now in the Bodleian library in Oxford. Many of the farms, fields and other features have survived almost unchanged so the landscape we see today would have been recognised by people from the time of the first Queen Elizabeth. The map goes into fascinating detail, even showing the use of each field – light green for pasture, green stripes for crops and so on. The same farms are still there and research has shown they often have structures dating from this time behind their more modern facades.

Have a look at the end walls of barns belonging to Harpsden Court Farm opposite the church, they contain old wooden blocks once used to print wallpaper.

6. Opposite two roads on the left turn right on a footpath called Peppard Lane. At the end of the path keep ahead to a main road.

7. Cross the road and continue along Mill Lane, a couple of yards to the right, as far as a car park on the left.

8. Turn left through the car park to a path on the far side. The path soon leads into an open area. Bear right to walk along the right-hand side. Continue through trees and eventually between fences.

9. Some 35 yards after the end of a building on the right, turn right to cross a stream at stepping stones. Follow the path to a gap on the right giving onto a car park. Turn right to the River and Rowing Museum and the teashop on the right.

The River and Rowing Museum has galleries devoted to the history of rowing, the river Thames, the history of Henley and the famous book about the creatures of the river, The Wind in the Willows, *as well as a changing programme of special exhibitions. It is open the same hours as the café.*

10. Leave the museum by the front entrance and go ahead to the river. Turn right, upstream. At a lane continue on the Thames Path, going out over the river on Marsh Lock then back to the river bank. Continue upstream. Stay on the waymarked Thames Path when it leaves the river bank and shortly joins a drive, which eventually becomes more of a road.

Marsh Lock is unusual, with long tow path bridges leading out to the lock island and back to the shore. The first lock was built by Humphrey Gainsborough, brother of the famous artist and minister of the Independent Chapel in Henley. He also

Marsh Lock.

superintended rebuilding the road up Remenham Hill, for which he invented a new system of rail trolleys.

11. Next to a house called Rivermead House bear right on a path waymarked as the Thames Path and follow this to a road. Turn right a few yards back to Shiplake station car park.

Walk 12
DINTON PASTURES

A walk round disused gravel pits on the outskirts of Reading hardly sounds inspiring, but this easy, level ramble is a little gem. The gravel workings have been flooded to make attractive lakes and Nature has healed the scars of extraction. The route is all on well-made paths, apart from a short stretch on a quiet lane, and so is suitable for all times of year.

The Dragonfly Café occupies the old farmhouse, built in 1904. It has a large, pleasant garden with several tables so you can enjoy tea outside in fine weather. It serves a range of delicious cakes such as coffee cake with ginger buttercream filling. Breakfast is served until noon and for lunch there is a wide selection of sandwiches, with soup if you wish, and filled jacket potatoes, as well as tempting daily specials. It is open from 10 am until 5 pm throughout the year. Telephone: 01189 321071.

DISTANCE: 3 miles.

MAP: OS Explorer 159 Reading.

STARTING POINT: Sandford Copse car park (GR 777730) for the Berkshire Museum of Aviation and Dinton Pastures Country Park. It is accessed from Mohawk Way, Woodley.

HOW TO GET THERE: From the Winersh Triangle junction on the A329(M), between the M4 and Reading, follow the signs for Woodley and Sonning. Turn right at a roundabout, signed 'Sandford Aviation Museum' and to a car park on the right.

ALTERNATIVE STARTING POINT: If you wish to visit the teashop at the beginning or end of your walk, start in the main car park for Dinton Pastures Country Park, reached from the B3030 Winnersh to Hurst road. The teashop is by the car park. You will then start the walk at point 6.

THE WALK

Berkshire Museum of Aviation is dedicated to the contribution the county has made to flying. A Second World War hangar has been moved here from Woodley Airfield ¹/₂ mile away and there are presently nine aircraft that represent Berkshire aviation over the last 60 years, including several built at Woodley. It is open from late March to the end of October on Wednesday, Saturday and Sunday and bank holidays between 10.30 am and 5 pm and between noon and 4 pm on Sundays in winter.

1. Go to the right-hand side of the car park and take a path that leads between the Air Training Corps building and a road. Ignore a small path on the left and follow the main path by the road for a few yards and then as it bears left downhill.

2. Bear right to cross a concrete bridge over a stream as a path joins from the left, soon walking by the river Loddon.

The Saxons called this area 'Whistley', which means marshy meadows in a woodland clearing. It was a Saxon stronghold when the Vikings held Reading and given by the king to the great abbey at Abingdon (see walk 19). Fish, mainly eels, were sent in great quantity to the abbey's kitchen and oak exported via the Loddon and the Thames to make choir stalls. From the 13th century onwards the parish was called Hurst. However, Hurst Gravel Pits is not an attractive name and the country park was called Dinton Pastures from the dairy farm that was here before gravel extraction started. Gravel was taken from the meadow by the river and the area was restored once this had ceased.

3. A few yards after a path joins on the right, turn left over a bridge

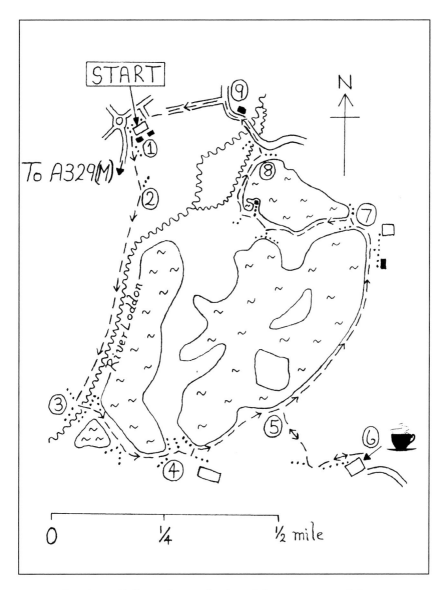

across the river. Follow the path ahead, between two lakes.

The gravelly soil from here has been used in road repairs for a long time. Extraction on a large scale happened between 1969 and 1979 to build parts of the M4 and A329(M). A condition of planning permission was that the area would be

The river Loddon.

landscaped when the extraction was complete: the result is an attractive and popular country park with several lakes.

4. At the end of the lake on the left, continue ahead past two paths on the left then turn left over a wooden footbridge to the edge of another lake. Turn right by the lake.

 5. At a picnic area, turn right away from the lake. Immediately after crossing a stream, bear left at a fork to pass to the left of a car park to the teashop.

The arrival of the Great Western Railway in the middle of the 19th century vastly improved communications and meant that milk for London could be produced some distance away: the line was nicknamed 'the milky way', from the number of churns carried. Dinton Pastures became a specialised dairy farm and the teashop is accommodated in the farmhouse, built in 1904.

6. Return to the lake and turn right. Continue round the lake, passing the Black Swan Sailing Club. Do not cross the bridge just after the sailing club but continue on the main path round the lake.

This is Black Swan Lake. The Emm Brook used to flow where the lake is now and helped drain the fields in winter. It was diverted during the extraction and now runs between the lake and the golf course. The oaks on the island in the lake were once on the banks of the stream. Unwanted soil was used to build up this area during gravel extraction; the golf course is 10 feet higher than the lake on average.

7. Some 50 yards after crossing a wooden footbridge turn right across another one. Turn left after a further 20 yards, now walking with yet another lake, Sandford Lake, on your right. Continue in the same direction when a broad path joins from the left. When the path forks, bear right to continue round the lake.

An obvious path on the right leads to a hide for bird watching overlooking the lake.

8. When the path bends right by a notice board, continue ahead to a gate onto a lane. Turn left.

9. Some 50 yards after Sandford Mill on the right, turn left along a lane, signed as a 'No Through Road'. When this ends at a turning space, continue ahead on a path past some bollards, back to the start.

A mill has stood here for centuries. An earlier building was destroyed by the Roundheads during the Civil War for supplying flour to the Royalists. The Harrisons of Hurst House were strong supporters of Charles I and as a consequence lost most of their wealth.

Walk 13
DORNEY AND THE
JUBILEE RIVER

If you enjoy waterside walking this route should come at the top of your list as it visits the Jubilee river, as well as a beautiful reach of the river Thames. The going is very easy, mostly on excellent paths, and is almost completely level. There is one tiny climb of a few metres and this miniscule effort is rewarded by an excellent view across the Thames Valley to Windsor Forest.

 The Walled Garden Centre at Dorney Court has an attractive modern interior and lots of tables outside in a garden shaded by mature trees. It offers a good selection of cakes such as banofee slice and chocolate cake, as well as cream teas. For lunch there is a wide selection of sandwiches, baguettes and filled jacket potatoes or a daily special such as, on my visit, beef stew and dumplings with all the trimmings. They are open all year from 9 am until 4.45 pm, just opening an hour later on Sunday. Telephone: 01628 669999.

DISTANCE: 5½ miles.
MAP: OS Explorer 160 Windsor, Weybridge & Bracknell.
STARTING POINT: Boveney car park (GR 938777).
HOW TO GET THERE: From the A4, Maidenhead to Slough road ½ mile west of junction 7 on the M4, take the B3026, signed 'Dorney 1½ Eton Wick 3 Eton 4' for 1½ miles. Turn right along Boveney Road, signed 'Boveney ¾' to a car park on the right opposite Old Place Cottage.
ALTERNATIVE STARTING POINT: If you wish to visit the teashop at the beginning or end of your walk, start at the Walled Garden Centre at Dorney Court where there is a large car park, though permission should be sought before leaving a car for an extended period. You will then start the walk at point 7.

THE WALK

1. Return to the lane and turn right. When the lane shortly ends at The Old Place continue ahead over a cattle grid on a surfaced track for 100 yards.

2. Turn left on a signed path along the left-hand side of a field. At the far end of the field follow the path round to the right for 150 yards to a footbridge on the left onto the open expanse of Dorney Common.

3. There is no defined path across the common but head slightly left, crossing a road, to find a gate just to the right of farm buildings. Through the gate continue ahead on a signed path over a slight rise, with a seat well-positioned to admire the view, and carry on to a cross path.

4. Turn left on a signed bridleway to a T-junction with another bridleway.

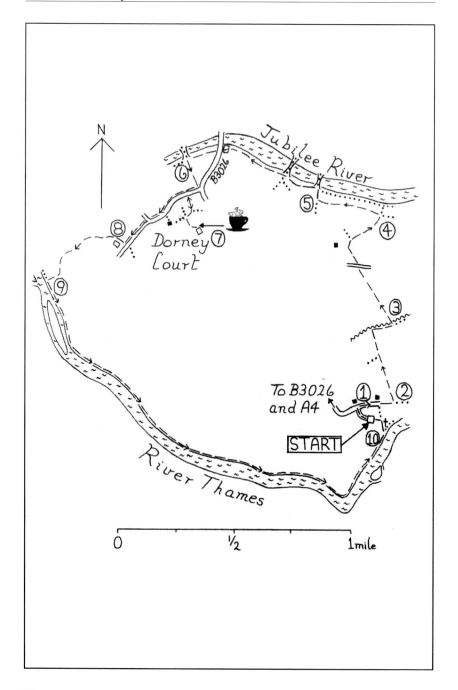

5. Turn right towards a footbridge. Do not cross the bridge but turn left beside the Jubilee river along a cycleway. Cross a road and carry on along the cycleway to the next footbridge.

Jubilee river is a flood alleviation scheme designed to reduce the risk of flooding in Maidenhead, Windsor and Eton: when the water level in the river Thames is high, gates at Taplow can be opened to divert water into the channel. It is seven miles long, took five years to build and was officially opened in 2002. The surrounding meadows and wetlands are the home of many species of wildlife and large flocks of birds spend the winter here.

6. Turn left through a wooden gate and walk along the left-hand side of a field to a stile onto a road. Turn right along the cycleway on the right-hand side of the road for 100 yards to the entrance to Dorney Court. Turn left along the drive to the Walled Garden Centre and teashop.

Dorney, which was mentioned in the Domesday Book, means island of bees, and honey is still produced locally. Dorney Court has been the home of the Palmer family for more than 450 years, passing from father to son through thirteen generations. A Grade 1 listed building, it is open to the public every August afternoon except Saturday, and the May Bank Holiday Monday and the preceding Sunday. The very first pineapple to be raised in England was grown at Dorney Court and presented to Charles II in 1661. From late April until the end of May, Dorney Court sells its own homegrown asparagus from the back entrance of the house. This is picked first thing every morning and has usually sold out by early afternoon. Telephone: 01628 604638.

7. Retrace your steps to the cycleway beside the road and turn left. Continue ahead when this joins the road. As the road turns right, keep on in the same direction on a path to the right of the entrance drive to Eton Boating Centre.

8. Stay on the path as it turns right away from the drive and follow it as it wends its way to the river Thames.

Dorney Lake, set in a 400-acre park with a Nature Conservation area, is a 2,200 m, eight-lane course with a separate return lane constructed to international standards by Eton College. It hosted the Rowing World

Dorney Court.

Championships in 2006. During the bid to host the 2012 Games, funding was provided to build a new finishing tower at the course and 30,000 spectators will be able to enjoy the Olympic rowing and flatwater canoe events here.

9. Turn left on the riverside path for about 2 miles.

10. At a small church take a signed path on the left, passing to the left of the church, to a gate on the left into the car park where this walk started.

The little chapel of St Mary Magdalene was built in the 1100s near a busy wharf to serve the bargees who plied their trade on the river. It is now disused and looked after by the Friends of Friendless Churches. Note the little slivers of flint pressed into the mortar lines, a technique known as galletting.

Walk 14
PANGBOURNE AND
MAPLEDURHAM LOCK

The Thames between Pangbourne and Purley is one of the loveliest stretches of the river and this route covers it in the right direction to enjoy the best views. The walk starts in Purley and wends its way by fields and woods to meet the little river Pang, a tributary of the Thames, which it follows into the riverside town of Pangbourne and the first opportunity for tea. This is followed by the outstanding stretch of river bank walking referred to above as far as Mapledurham Lock and the second opportunity for refreshment, leaving just a short inland section, with some more excellent views, back to the start.

The Jolly Good Food Company lives up to its name in all respects and is very popular with locals at lunchtime in this busy community. There is a particularly good choice of cakes including, on my visit, a truly outstanding lemon and blueberry cream sponge one of the best slices of cake I have ever enjoyed (and I have tasted quite a few!). For lunch there is an excellent range of sandwiches and baguettes supplemented by soup of the day. They are open every day except Sunday between 8 am and 5 pm and some Sunday mornings. Telephone: 0118 9842246.

Mapledurham Lock is in an outstanding position and is beautifully kept. Teas with delicious cakes and biscuits are served between 10 am and 6 pm at weekends from Easter, all through the summer from May until the end of October and every day during the school summer holidays. In addition, pictures by four local artists are on display. Many are of local scenes through the year and make a unique souvenir of a lovely walk. Telephone: 0118 9417776.

DISTANCE: 7 miles.

MAP: OS Explorer 171 Chiltern Hills West.

STARTING POINT: The parking place immediately west of Purley on the A329 (GR 652762). If this is full, there is room to leave a car without causing inconvenience in Beech Road, 100 yards towards Purley.

HOW TO GET THERE: Purley is on the A329, the Wantage road out of Reading. Immediately west of Purley, just by a 50mph sign, there is a parking place marked with a blue 'P'.

ALTERNATIVE STARTING POINT: If you wish to visit the teashop in Pangbourne at the beginning or end of your walk, start in the long stay car park near the river. To find the teashop turn left out of the car park into the centre of Pangbourne and the teashop is to the left. You will then start the walk at point 13. There is no public parking at Mapledurham Lock.

THE WALK

1. Facing the road, turn right for 100 yards then turn right up Beech Road. When the road bends sharp left, take a signed path on the right, between house numbers 5 and 7.

2. Cross a wooden squeeze stile then follow the path left to the top of a field. Fork left into a strip of woodland and follow the path through the trees and ahead to a second wood.

3. Just inside the second wood, turn left and continue on the path as it soon leaves the wood, walking with the trees on the right. When the wood ends, follow the path as it bears left. Go over a clear cross path and carry on to a lane.

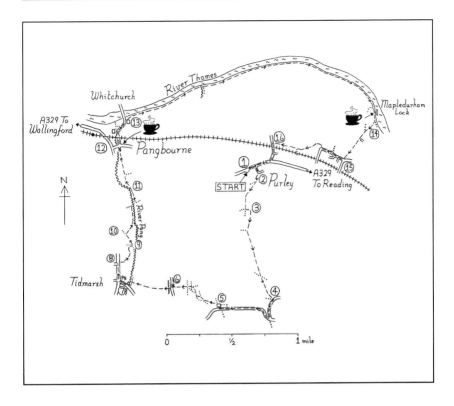

4. Turn right. At a road junction, turn right, signed 'Sulham 1 Tidmarsh 1½', and continue as far as a car park for Sulham Woods.

5. Go through a wooden barrier on the left-hand side of the car park and follow the main path, marked by a yellow arrow. Ignore a path on the left then after a further 60 yards, turn left, signed as a public footpath. Stay on the main path, defined for a while by planks of wood then bearing left downhill to a stile out of the wood. Go on down the left-hand side of a field to a lane, the stile being a few yards right from the corner.

6. Turn left along the lane for 30 yards to a path on the right to a wooden footbridge. Walk along the right-hand side of the first field and the left-hand side of a second field, passing some World War II pillboxes used as cow sheds, to a track. Cross the track and a footbridge to soon reach a lane.

There are many pillboxes dotted about the countryside of the Thames Valley. During the Second World War, when the threat of German invasion was very real, the Thames was designated the line of defence behind which the defensive forces would retreat if the Channel coast was taken and provision was made to blow up every bridge over the river.

7. Turn right to a road junction and right again for about 250 yards.

This road through Tidmarsh was built as a turnpike in coaching days and so this has long been a busy village. In common with many other villages, it used to be much more self sufficient with its own bakery and other shops, post office, school and mill. The latter was certainly in operation by the 13th century and continued until the early years of the 20th. There was also a vineyard here in the 13th century.

8. Just after Strachey Close on the left, turn right on a signed path that leads between hedges and fences to a surfaced drive.

9. Turn left to immediately meet a surfaced track on a bend and go straight on until the track ends at two field gates, each with a stile beside it.

10. Cross the stile on the right and go along the right-hand side of two small fields to meet the river Pang. Follow the path with the river on your right and then cross it at a footbridge to continue in the same direction on the other bank.

 11. When the river bends left, go straight ahead to a gate onto a fenced path that eventually leads into an unsurfaced lane with houses on both sides. Follow this into Pangbourne and turn right for a few yards then cross the road at the zebra crossing to the teashop.

Pangbourne is an ancient settlement, which grew up at an important crossing of the river. The Roman road from Silchester to Dorchester crossed here and Neolithic, Roman and Saxon remains have been found locally. The parish church, rebuilt in 1868, is on land granted by Beorhtwulf, King of Mercia, in AD 843. The heyday of this riverside town was in Edwardian times when boating on the Thames was at the height of its popularity. The three men (not forgetting the dog) whose rowing trip up from London is so hilariously described by Jerome K. Jerome finally gave up at Pangbourne and slunk off back to the restaurants and theatres of the capital. Pangbourne is also closely associated with Kenneth Grahame's classic 'The Wind in the Willows'. 'Believe me, my young friend, there is nothing – absolutely nothing –

The river Pang.

half so much worth doing as simply messing about in boats', describes Grahame's own pleasure. The landscape of the book is an imaginary one with elements of all the rivers the author knew and loved. He lived by the Thames at Cookham Dean with his grandmother after his mother died when he was five. Later on he knew the Thames at Oxford and the Fal and Fowey in Cornwall from holidays there. The story is not so much about animals but a group of Edwardian gentlemen of leisure leading a carefree existence on the river that Grahame, who worked in the Bank of England, would have enjoyed. The Thames was not fixed as the setting until illustrations were being prepared for a new edition in 1930. By then Grahame was living in Pangbourne and pointed out various spots in the locality to the artist, E. H. Shepard.

12. After tea, turn right out of the teashop. Take the first right signed 'Whitchurch via toll bridge B471'. Bear right through a long stay car park to the river Thames.

Like Goring and Streatley (see walk 16), Pangbourne and Whitchurch are twin communities on either side of the river, linked by one of only two toll bridges remaining on the river. Tolls were once charged to cross nearly all the bridges over the river, not only by private individuals but also councils. Both categories were too

Mapledurham Lock.

often content to rake in as much money as they could and spend as little as possible on repairs. In many cases, the tolls were so onerous they were a serious impediment to the movement of goods and people. A study has been done of the incidence of marriages between the young people of Whitchurch and Pangbourne before and after the bridge was built in 1793. There was no increase in cross river romance, suggesting that the tolls were a real deterrent.

13. Turn right and follow the river downstream to Mapledurham Lock and the second opportunity for tea.

Mapledurham, across the river and not accessible from this side, comprises a Tudor manor house with a 15th-century church, mill and cottages. It is the ancestral home of the Blount family, staunchly Roman Catholic so the house boasts a priest's hole and secret passages. The church, though Anglican, has a Catholic chapel. This arrangement was disputed to no avail by a Victorian rector with the wonderful name of Lord Augustus FitzClarence. He was one of William IV's ten illegitimate children with his mistress, the actress Mrs Jordan (see walk 2). Two 18th-century daughters of the Blount family, Martha and Teresa, were noted beauties. Teresa retired from society after George I's coronation in 1714:

She went to plain work, and to purling brooks,
Old fashioned halls, dull aunts, and croaking rooks,
She went from opera, park, assembly, play,
to morning walks and prayers three times a day.

Mapledurham House is the inspiration for Toad Hall in the illustrated edition of 'The Wind in the Willows' referred to above.

14. Immediately after the lock turn right, away from the river, to a gate giving onto a track. Turn left to reach a road.

Purley is now for all practical purposes a suburb of Reading, having grown from a riverside village with a population of about 200 in the 19th century.

15. Turn right. When the road bends left, turn right on a public bridleway. Follow this across a track to a lane.

16. Turn left, over a railway, to the main road. Turn right, back to the start.

Walk 15
DENHAM AND THE GRAND UNION CANAL

This easy short walk explores the waterways that criss-cross part of the Colne Valley. In just three short miles it visits the river Colne, an important tributary of the mighty Thames, Frays river and the Grand Union Canal. The route starts in the charming village of Denham and wends its way to a welcoming waterside tea garden. The walk is almost entirely level and there is no road except through the interesting village.

Fran's Tea Garden is to be found where Frays river passes beneath the canal at Denham Lock and is particularly popular with walkers and cyclists. There is a good selection of cakes; the apple cake, made to an old family recipe, is delicious. For a light lunch there is a choice of sandwiches or filled jacket potatoes. Fran's is open every day except Monday and Tuesday (open Bank Holidays) throughout the year. However, Fran does sometimes take a couple of week's holiday in the depths of the winter so it is wise to phone and check she will be open. The hours are 10 am until 6.30 pm from the beginning of May until the end of September and until 3.30 pm in the winter. There is no indoor seating though there are some tables undercover. Telephone: 01895 271070.

When Fran's is closed Colne Valley Visitor Centre serves light refreshments and has toilets. There are also pubs in Denham that serve food.

DISTANCE: 3 miles.
MAP: OS Explorer 172 Chiltern Hills East.
STARTING POINT: St Mary's church, Denham (GR 043870).
HOW TO GET THERE: From the M40, junction 1, take the A40 west towards Gerrards Cross. Almost immediately turn right, signed 'Village only', along Old Mill Road to Denham Village. There are several parkings spots by the church. Alternatively, go by train to Denham station and take the path under the railway to pick up the route at point 2.
ALTERNATIVE STARTING POINT: It is not posssible to start at the teashop as it is not accessible by road.

THE WALK

1. Continue ahead through the village, passing the Swan and the Green Man. As the main road bends left, continue ahead to the gates of Denham Place then turn right along The Pyghtle. When the surfaced lane ends, ignore a path on the right and carry on along the surfaced path ahead.

The core of the old village is charming and little changed since the beginning of the last century. There are three pubs grouped around the village green. They should be good because the parish also contains a development of retirement homes for Licensed Victuallers. There have been many famous visitors down the years since one Ulstan gave the manor to Westminster Abbey in the 11th century. They have changed from convalescing nuns in the 12th century to film people from nearby Denham studios in the 20th. Henry III granted a charter for a weekly market and an annual three-day fair. The latter survives today, now a one-day event held on the second Bank Holiday in May. Denham Place, glimpsed through its imposing gates, was built for Sir Roger Hill between 1688 and 1701 at a cost of £5,591 16s 9d.

2. When the surfaced path bends left there are a footpath and bridleway on the right. Take the bridleway, not the path through a metal gate, to walk with a wire fence on the left.

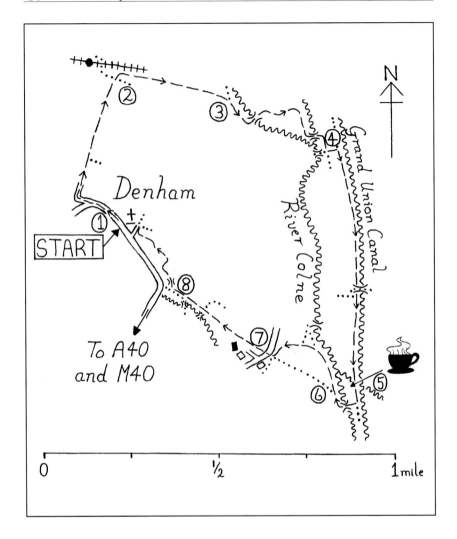

3. When the path reaches a river near a magnificent, grey brick viaduct turn right to follow the path over the river at a footbridge and on through woods to a second footbridge. Press ahead along the path for 100 yards.

This is the river Colne. It rises at London Colney in Hertfordshire and enters the Thames at Staines. For much of its length the river is the boundary between Buckinghamshire and the London Borough of Hillingdon.

The Grand Union Canal.

4. Take a path on the left, more or less opposite a gate on the right, which gives onto another footbridge. The path shortly leads to the Grand Union Canal. Turn right along the towpath to the teashop on the right at Denham Lock.

Teams of men known as navigators or navvies built the canal in the great era of canal construction in the early 19th century. It was part of a series of independent but connected waterways. They were combined in 1928, hence the name 'Grand Union'. In 1832 it was reported that 100 barges a week, drawn by relays of horses, used this canal, carrying over 15 tons of manufactured goods to London. The advent of the railways reduced this flow of goods to almost nothing and pleasure boats are now the main traffic. Denham Lock is the deepest one on the canal. Just before the lock a river flows under the canal. This is Frays river. It is not a natural water course but was dug, perhaps following the course of a stream, to provide water to power mills in the Uxbridge area. One of these mills was owned by a Mr Frays, hence the correct name of Frays river, not river Frays. When the canal was built the flow was maintained by the construction of an aqueduct to carry the canal.

5. Turn right out of the teashop and continue along the tow path for

100 yards. Turn right and cross a footbridge over the river Colne. Across the bridge follow the main path to the right to a fork.

6. Bear right, not left through a wooden gate, to continue by the river. As the path approaches a wooden footbridge, bear left on the main path away from the river and walk along this to a gate on the right onto a drive.

7. Cross the drive to a similar gate and follow the path past Colne Valley Visitor Centre to a gate onto a path beside a golf course. When the fence on the right ends, press on in the same direction, across a surfaced path then a green to pick up the fence on the left and continue beside it.

Colne Valley Regional Park was established in 1965 to manage the area that extends from Staines to Chorleywood, the first real countryside on London's western edge. It is a mosaic of farmland, woods and wetlands, criss-crossed by waterways and has several country parks along its length. One of them, Denham, has been explored on this walk. The Visitor Centre is managed by Groundwork, a charitable trust that works with local people to improve the environment, and provides facilities for the whole park.

8. Do not go through gates ahead onto the road but turn right over yet another footbridge. Follow the fenced path to a lane. Cross the lane and cut through the churchyard back to the start.

Walk 16
GORING AND THE RIDGEWAY

This superb walk, the longest in the book, makes a wonderful all-day expedition with a packed lunch, tea in Goring and a drink at the famous Beetle and Wedge to round it off. It starts by climbing onto the Berkshire Downs and there are some excellent long distance views across the Thames to the Chilterns beyond. It then joins the Ridgeway for the descent to the twin villages of Streatley and Goring before returning by the river to the start, passing one of the most famous hotels on the Thames.

Jan Marie bakery in the small modern shopping arcade is popular with local people and a good place for lunch because, as a bakers, it opens early at 7 am and closes similarly early at 3.30 pm Monday to Friday and opens and closes an hour later on Saturday. It is closed on Sunday. At lunchtime there is a good choice of filled baguettes and sandwiches or salad and soup of the day. There is a tempting choice of cakes and pastries from the selection sold in the shop. There are some tables outside. Telephone: 01491 874264.

When the teashop is closed there are several pubs in Goring that serve food, notably the historic Miller of Mansfield and the Catherine Wheel.

DISTANCE: 8½ miles.
MAP: OS Explorer 170 Abingdon, Wantage & Vale of White Horse and 171 Chiltern Hills West.
STARTING POINT: Moulsford Recreation Ground car park. This is by the telephone kiosk and bus stop on the A329 (GR 591838).
HOW TO GET THERE: Moulsford is on the A329 between Reading and Wallingford.
ALTERNATIVE STARTING POINT: If you wish to visit the teashop at the beginning or end of your walk, start in Goring where there is ample parking in the signed car park. The teashop is on the High Street, to the right of the path from the car park. You will then start the walk at point 10.

THE WALK

1. Leave the back of the car park and walk along the right-hand side of the recreation ground to a gap in the hedge. Cross a field to another gap but do not go through it. Instead, turn left to walk with the hedge on your right. At the end of the field, turn right on a cross path that heads up the right-hand side of a field, under some pylons, to a road.

2. Turn right for 40 yards then turn left along the drive to Starveall Farm, signed as a footpath. Continue past the farm as the drive becomes a rough track. Stay on the track, ignoring paths and tracks on the right and left. As you climb beside a wood take plenty of opportunities to admire the ever widening view. After a while the track starts to descend.

3. When the track turns sharp left, continue ahead on a grassy path, forking left towards a wood after 60 yards. Follow the path through the wood to reach a cross track.

4. Turn right and continue.

5. At a T junction with a cross track, continue ahead on a signed grassy path through woods to emerge on a track by a house.

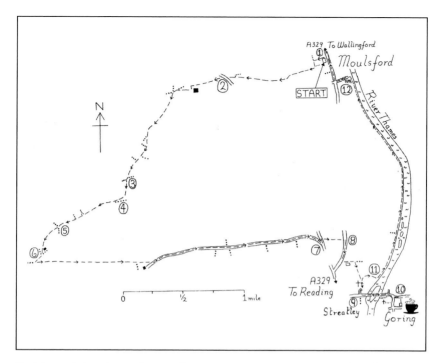

6. Turn right along the track, soon meeting a cross track. This is the Ridgeway. Turn left and follow it downhill, continuing as it becomes a narrow lane after Warren Farm, to a main road.

The Ridgeway, one of the great trade routes of Europe, has probably been in use for 4,000 years and is one of the oldest roads in the world. It runs from the Dorset coast to the North Sea and rides the back of one of the six great ridges that radiate from Salisbury Plain. It is thought that this ancient route followed the high chalk land to avoid thick forest and marsh and prehistoric remains are found in abundance along its length. Keeping company with the Ridgeway for some of its journey, but at a lower level, is another ancient highway, the Icknield Way, which came into being later than the Ridgeway. The Ridgeway, on top of chalk hills, had no water which is why there are no villages on it today. The Icknield Way runs nearer to the spring line so giving travellers easier access to water. It came into use later when, presumably, there were fewer dangers from wolves and other wild animals in the woods.

The Ridgeway Path is a modern creation. It was proposed by the Ramblers' Association in 1942 and brought into being by the Countryside Commission as a long distance route from Ivinghoe Beacon in Buckinghamshire to Overton Hill in Wiltshire. In part it runs along the ancient Ridgeway but also uses other paths.

The Ridgeway.

As you walk along this ancient road, look to your left. The overhead power lines and pylons that support them suddenly go underground. This is to protect the spectacular views across Goring Gap to the Chilterns beyond from their ugly intrusion.

7. Turn left for 40 yards then right along Townsend Road (an unadopted road that is not made up) and follow this to another road.

8. Turn right for about 200 yards then left on a surfaced drive to Cleeve Court, signed as a public footpath. After 150 yards turn right along a signed footpath. Walk along this to join a track and continue in the same direction, behind a church, to a road.

Streatley means 'the glade by the Roman road', showing how long there have been people living here. A century ago it had a population of just under a thousand, served by a grocer, miller, baker, draper, tailor, cobbler and several other trades. The population is still much the same but now it is more of a very pleasant dormitory community and nothing like so self sufficient.

 9. Turn left and walk over the double bridge into Goring.

Continue along the main road through Goring to the teashop on the right.

Goring and Streatley grew up at this important ford across the Thames. Before the first bridge was built about 100 years ago, the two towns were linked by a ferry and a ford. In 1674 a ferry capsized and all 60 people on board were drowned. On the other hand, Goring seems good for your health. In the church is a memorial to one Hugh Whistler who died in 1615 aged 216! (Before you make immediate arrangements to move to Goring, you should know that the 2 and the 1 are thought to be a badly carved 4.)

The Miller of Mansfield inn is a mixture of three buildings - a 17th-century brick and flint wing, the main block is Georgian and there are Victorian additions. It is a very popular resting place with people walking the Ridgeway. The name is supposed to derive from an early inn keeper who came from Sherwood Forest. King Henry II was out hunting and became separated from his party. He begged a bed and meal from a miller who had no idea of his guest's identity. His wife served what she called a 'lightfoot pastry' and the King remarked that it tasted like venison, which of course it couldn't be since all deer belonged to the King and poaching them was such a serious offence. The miller said that what the King didn't know wouldn't harm him and that he had several carcasses in the roof. The next day the rest of the hunting party found the King and the miller saw the noose beckon. However, the King was so grateful for the miller's generosity that he let him off, on condition that he continued to provide hospitality to weary travellers. It makes a good story anyway!

10. Retrace your steps over the bridges and turn right to walk again on the track behind the church. Now fork right, signed 'Thames Path', to the river bank.

11. Turn left, upstream, and follow the river bank for about $1^{1}/_{2}$ miles, passing Cleve Lock, to the Beetle and Wedge.

A beetle is a large, heavy mallet used to drive a wedge into wood to split it into planks for floating downriver to London. H.G. Wells stayed at this famous pub while writing 'The History of Mr Polly' and it is said to have inspired his description of the Potwell Inn in the novel. Though the pub may have changed, we can all recognise Mr Polly's enthusiasm as he approaches a source of refreshment!

12. Turn left through the hotel car park and along a lane to the main road. Turn right for about $^{1}/_{4}$ mile, back to the start.

Walk 17
WALLINGFORD AND BENSON

This short, easy ramble starts in the ancient borough of Wallingford, once one of the most important towns in England, with a long and interesting history. You can visit the remains of the once mighty castle before following quiet tracks and field paths to the Thames near Benson. The return leg is a level stroll by the river, using the Thames Path.

 The Waterside Cafe at Benson is one of the very few places where it is possible to have tea overlooking the river. It is a modern building, with extensive outdoor seating, and next to a boatyard just above Benson Lock. This means there is plenty of entertainment to be had in watching the river traffic come and go. As well as excellent cakes, the Waterside Cafe also serves an outstanding all-day breakfast so, if you time your walk carefully, you can do as I did and combine the two best meals to eat in England - breakfast and tea - and call it brunch, or perhaps that should be brea! There is an extensive choice for lunch and it is very popular with locals, as well as the boating fraternity. In addition to full meals including daily specials, it offers a tempting selection of sandwiches and baguesttes with chunky chips and innovative salads such as 'The Morning' which comprises a salad of bacon and black pudding on baby leaves. It is open throughout the year from 8 am. Telephone: 01491 833732.

DISTANCE: 3½ miles.

MAP: OS Explorer 171 Chiltern Hills West.

STARTING POINT: Thames Street car park, Wallingford (fee payable Monday to Saturday) (GR 608894). If this car park is full, continue along Thames Street to a second signed car park.

HOW TO GET THERE: Follow the signs to Wallingford from the A4074, the Oxford to Reading road, at the junction with the A4130, the Henley-on-Thames road. Cross the bridge and take the first road on the left, Thames Street, to a car park on the right.

ALTERNATIVE STARTING POINT: If you wish to visit the teashop at the beginning or end of your walk, start at Benson. The car park at the teashop is too small to leave your car there whilst you walk but it should be possible to find a suitable spot nearby, notably on the lane between points 6 and 7. You will then start the walk at point 7, walking downriver from the teashop to cross Benson Lock.

THE WALK

Wallingford is a Saxon town laid out in the late 9th or early 10th century and the basic street plan still survives as do some of the earthworks, built by Alfred the Great or his son Edward against a threatened Danish attack. At that time, Wallingford was an important place with its own mint, much larger than Oxford and about equal in size to Winchester, Alfred's capital. After the Conquest it remained a busy centre of affairs but declined after the 14th century until at one time there were only 44 houses. It settled into life as a market town with some fascinating corners to explore. An outstanding walking guide has been produced by Wallingford Historical and Archaeological Society, available from the Tourist Information Centre at the Town Hall in the Market Square, open on Monday to Saturday between 10 am and 4 pm, also on Sundays from mid-July to the end of August. Telephone: 01491 826972.

The church on Thames Street, St Peter's, has an unusual open fluted spire, which was highly controversial when it was built in the 18th century on the site of a former church destroyed in the siege during the Civil War. It was paid for by Sir William Blackstone, a famous judge of the time whose 'Commentaries on the Laws of England' was a major influence on the American Constitution. The same man caused the line of Thames Street to be moved to the west to enlarge his garden so the straight Saxon way now has a kink!

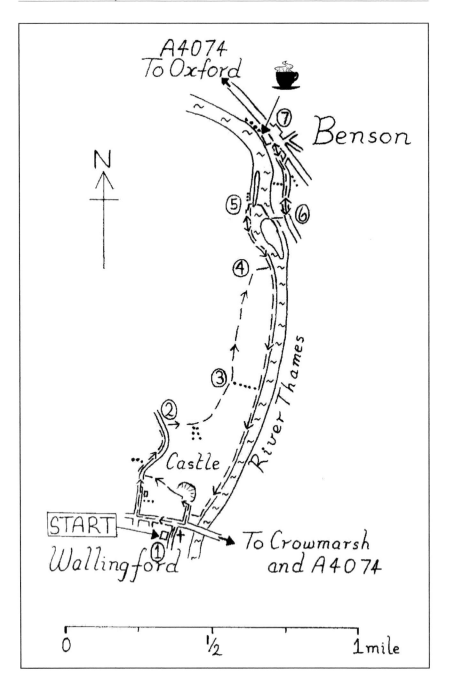

The castle grounds are open between 10 am and 6 pm April to October and well worth taking the time to explore, especially for the fine view from the top of the motte. A visit to the castle does involve walking through the town, though, which otherwise can be bypassed.

Note: *The castle and its grounds are not accessible from Castle Lane, which follows the line of the inner moat defending the base of the motte. It was lined with clay and, to this day, Castle Lane tends to be very wet.*

1. From the car park, turn left along Thames Street.

*If you wish to visit the castle, turn **left** at the main road, then right along Castle Street. The entrance to the castle grounds is on the right. After visiting the castle, return to Castle Street and turn right along the road as far as the cemetery on the right. You will then be at point 2 of the walk.*

The green mounds and fragments of masonry are all that remain of what was once one of the strongest and most important castles in England where momentous affairs of state took place. William the Conqueror thought the strategic importance of Wallingford was so great that he took the town on his way to London and ordered the building of a substantial castle. The first phase, the motte and bailey, was completed by 1071 and it was extended several times during the subsequent centuries. From the top of the motte there are extensive views in all directions. A small section of wall on the river side was traditionally part of the Queen's Tower and another fragment to the north shows the extent of the 11th-century Inner Bailey. The most extensive wall left standing was part of the King's chapel inside the castle. As you follow the path to the modern bridge over Castle Lane, you are crossing the once bustling Middle Bailey, built in the 13th century. Excavations in 1972 revealed the remains of some 12th-century mud and straw houses covered when the Middle Bailey was built.

Note: At the time of writing, the bridge to the motte is closed as it has become unsafe but I am assured that there are plans to rebuild it shortly.

The heyday of Wallingford Castle's importance was between the 11th and 14th centuries. It was Queen Matilda's stronghold in the civil war between her and King Stephen who besieged it three times without success. Peace between the warring factions was finally made here. Matilda's son, Henry II, held his first Great Council at the castle in 1155 and granted the town its first charter. Edward II gave the castle to his favourite, Piers Gaveston, in 1307 and made him Baron Wallingford. Gaveston spent huge sums of money on the castle and held munificent entertainments, attended by most of the court. After Gaveston was executed in 1313, Wallingford played a major role in the intrigues that led to the horrible killing of Edward II. One of the main conspirators was Edward's wife, Isabella, who later surrendered the castle to Edward III. Wallingford Castle continued as a royal

The Thames at Benson.

residence but by the 16th century had fallen into disrepair. It was robbed of stone and lead, shipped down river for the building of Windsor Castle, and its last glory was as a Royalist stronghold in the Civil War. It was fortified again and in 1646 was besieged by Cromwell's troops, holding out for 16 weeks before the Royalist troops marched out with flying colours to disband. It was used as a prison for a few years but in 1652 Cromwell ordered it to be 'slighted' or pulled down so it could never be used as a stronghold again.

If you are not visiting the castle, turn right at the main road, then left, next to the Town Arms, along Castle Lane. At Castle Lane House, turn left on a track and follow this to a road. Turn right using the footway on the opposite side, for just under $1/4$ mile to a cemetery on the right.

2. Some 50 yards after the main entrance to the cemetery, turn right on a signed foopath which is a surfaced track through the cemetery. Continue ahead at the end of the cemetery and follow the now unsurfaced path ahead between metal fences to a stile by a gate into a field.

3. Turn left and walk along the left-hand side of two fields. At the end of the field, turn right to the river.

4. Turn left, upstream, to just before Benson Lock.

5. Cross the lock and weir over the river Thames and follow the path to a lane.

6. Turn left. A path has been created to the right of the lane to enable you to avoid this bit of road walking but the path is so overgrown and the lane so quiet, it hardly seems worth using it. Continue in the same direction at a junction to a main road. Turn left on a signed path to the river. Go through a gate on the right to the teashop.

Benson, across the road, used to be an important coaching stop known as Bensington. A guide book written in the early years of the 20th century describes it as a sleepy place that modern times have passed by. That could not be said today because at the edge of the village is a large RAF station, which houses the Queen's Flight.

7. After tea, retrace your steps across Benson Lock to point 5 and turn left. Follow the path beside the river back to Wallingford. As the path approaches the bridge, follow it round to the right to Castle Lane. Turn left to the main road. Turn right, then the first left, Thames Street, to the car park where this walk started.

Wallingford has long been an important crossing point of the Thames and it is said that the first bridge over the river was built here. At 900 feet long it is only 15 feet shorter than the old London Bridge. Its maintenance was the responsibility of the Corporation of Wallingford and the rents from various properties in the town, the Bridge Estate, helped to pay for its upkeep as did the tolls that used to be levied. It has, of course, been rebuilt numerous times. However, some fragments of medieval construction remain: a few of the pointed 13th-century arches can be seen on the downstream side of the causeway towards Crowmarsh Gifford across the river.

Walk 18
LITTLE WITTENHAM AND DORCHESTER

This walk is exceptionally varied and interesting with something to please everyone. It starts with a climb to Wittenham Clumps from which there are wonderful views in all directions - well worth the effort! The route then drops down through woodland to the Thames and there is a stretch by the river before visiting the ancient town of Dorchester with its wealth of historic interest and tea. The last leg is an easy stroll through meadows back to Little Wittenham.

Dorchester Abbey Tea Rooms is most unusual. Situated in a former guest house, all the cakes are donated by local people and the profits support a wide range of charities both national and international. This means that the cakes on offer depend on what has been made by the people involved. Indoors the service is family-style, sat round large tables spread with plates of cakes and you pay for what you take, adding up your own bill. There is also a sheltered garden at the rear. Teas are served from 2.30 pm at the weekend on Saturday and Sunday and Bank Holiday Mondays from Easter until the end of September and on Wednesday and Thursday from mid May. Telephone 01865 340054.

When the teashop is closed there are several pubs in Dorchester that serve food.

DISTANCE: 6 miles.

MAP: OS Explorer 170 Abingdon, Wantage & Vale of White Horse and 171 Chiltern Hills West.

STARTING POINT: Little Wittenham church where there is some parking outside (GR 566935). If this is full, return to a car park passed coming from the A4130 (GR 567924). Take a path from the back of this car park and almost immediately fork right uphill. Follow the path into the trees crowning the hill and continue ahead when a path joins on the left, so joining the route at point 4. The disadvantage of this starting point is that the last part of the walk is the climb up to Wittenham Clumps.

HOW TO GET THERE: From the A4130 between Wallingford and Didcot, 3 miles west of Wallingford, take a minor road signed 'Wittenhams 1½ Appleford 3½'. After about ½ mile turn right, signed 'Wittenham Clumps ½ Little Wittenham 1', and follow this road to Little Wittenham church. Little Wittenham may also be reached from the A415 at Clifton Hampden, between Abingdon and Burcot, continuing via Long Wittenham.

ALTERNATIVE STARTING POINT: If you wish to visit the teashop at the beginning or end of your walk, start in Dorchester where there is a signed public car park across the road from the abbey. You will then start the walk at point 11.

THE WALK

Today, Little Wittenham is a peaceful backwater. The oldest part of St Peter's church is the tower, dating from the 14th and 15th centuries; the rest was reconstructed in the last century. The church has many memorials to the influential Dunch family. The founder of the family's fortunes was William Dunch, Auditor to the Mint in 1546 and granted the manor of Little Wittenham by Elizabeth I in 1562. There is a brass showing him and his wife and an elaborate effigy to his grandson, another William, who was MP for Wallingford and died in 1611, aged 33. This also commemorates his wife, Marie, who was a sister-in-law of John Hampden, the parliamentary leader, and aunt to Oliver Cromwell. The Dunches held the manor until 1719 and their manor house, just north of the village, was demolished soon after this date.

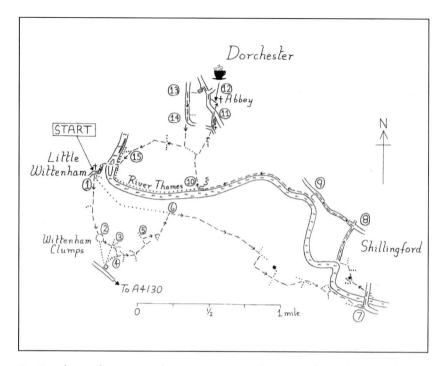

1. Go through a gate almost opposite the church and immediately bear right on a clear path leading to the top of the hill.

(If you do not want to climb the hill - well worth the effort for the stunning views - take the centre path to rejoin the route at point 6.)

These hills are properly the Sinodun Hills but are universally known as Wittenham Clumps due to the trees crowning their summits. It is said they are seen at their best under a full moon on a cloudless summer's night but on a clear day the views are outstanding. This first hill, Harp Hill, is the slightly higher of the two at 403 feet and was never fortified. To the west the Vale of White Horse can be seen on a clear day while the view to the north makes the strategic position of the hills obvious. To the south the view is bounded by the Berkshire Downs while eastwards the Chilterns can be seen. A view finder helps pick out the main features and, interestingly, does not mention Didcot Power Station which, depending on your attitude, lends dramatic contrast or is a dreadful blot on the landscape.

2. At the top turn left to walk round a wooded enclosure and at the far side turn left again to walk to the second clump, crossing a track from a car park.

The Poem Tree.

3. Some 15 yards after crossing a stile, the path forks. Bear right, across the ditch of the Iron Age fort, and up some steps. Head straight across a grassy area and into some trees crowning the hill.

The well-drained, easily cultivated soils by the important highway of the Thames were fought over for centuries and there was a fort on this strategically important hill before the Romans came, when the Atrebates to the north were battling the Catuvellauni to the south. A deep ditch was dug partway up the hill and the spoil used to construct ramparts behind it. The only entrance was on the south-west side of the hill, away from the river. A ditch on the eastern side was called the Money Pit and was believed to contain buried treasure, guarded by a ghostly raven!

4. At a T junction with a cross path turn left, soon leaving the trees and heading half left downhill to a stile. Continue about halfway down the left-hand side of a field to a stile on the left. Over this follow the path ahead down to a track.

Just as you leave the trees on Castle Hill note the massive stump of a dead beech on the right. This is the Poem Tree. It was the subject of some superior graffiti in the 19th century when Joseph Tubb inscribed a poem in its bark. This is hardly visible today, but there is a rendering on a stone just beyond the trees. You might find the first line of the poem particularly apposite.

5. Turn right and, ignoring tracks joining on the right, follow the track to a T junction with a cross track.

6. Some 250 yards before a farm, turn right, signed at the time of writing 'Diverted bridle path' for 200 yards. Turn left to pass the farm on the left and continue across a track to a T-junction with a farm drive. Cross the drive and carry on along a broad, grassy path to a metal field gate across the path. Immediately after the gate, turn left to the river, then right by the river to Shillingford Bridge.

Shillingford Bridge was constructed in 1827 in conjunction with a new turnpike road to Reading. Many think it is one of the most graceful bridges on the river.

7. Turn left over the bridge and at the end of the bridge turn left along a private road, signed 'Thames Path'. At the river turn right along a lane to a main road.

8. Turn left. Unfortunately, there is no way of avoiding walking along this stretch of busy main road but at least there is a footpath on the right.

9. Opposite the road sign for Dorchester, turn left on a path signed once more 'Thames Path', to the river. Turn right by the river and continue along the bank.

The Thames has always been a potential invasion route and defensive line. Note the pillbox on the right, one of many built in 1940-1 to hold the line of the Thames against the threatened German invasion.

10. Cross the bridge over the river Thame at the confluence of the two rivers and immediately turn right to follow a path and then a track across fields towards Dorchester. When the track joins a road, continue ahead in the same direction, soon passing a Catholic church on the right.

☕ **11.** At a main road cross over into the abbey grounds and the teashop is to the left of the church.

People have lived in this favoured spot for thousands of years. Just to the north west of the town was a Neolithic henge, now destroyed by gravel workings as were a number of Bronze Age barrows. This was a significant site in the Iron Age. The Romans built a fort here to control the river and the road from Winchester to Lincoln. When the legions left in the 5th century, the Saxons moved in. The most significant event in Dorchester's history occurred in AD 635. A Benedictine monk, Birinus, was sent by Pope Honorius to convert the West Saxons. He succeeded in his mission and baptised King Cynegils and his court in the Thame while the King of Northumbria looked on. Birinus stayed on as Bishop and Dorchester remained a cathedral city until after the Norman Conquest. In 1072 the bishopric moved to Lincoln and the church was given to the Augustinians in about 1140. Over the next 400 years they built the great abbey church over the Saxon cathedral. There is much of interest to see and it is well worth a visit. Most of the rest of the abbey disappeared after the Dissolution in 1536 and no doubt stones from the buildings are to be found in many local houses. The church endures because it was bought for £140 and given to the town as its parish church. The only other building to survive was the Guest House which houses the teashop and also contains a museum. It is open Tuesday to Saturday and Bank Holidays from 10.30 am to 12.30 pm and 2 pm to 5.30 pm. On Sundays it is just open in the afternoon. Admission is free.

12. From the teashop turn right, then right along the High Street. Turn left along Malthouse Lane. Turn right in front of a row of thatched cottages and continue in the same direction after the last cottage.

Dorchester presents a particularly attractive townscape with many 17th and 18th-century buildings. Until the bypass was opened in 1982, the traffic was dreadful and you may have noticed a tunnel on the right as you approached the abbey, which you formerly used to avoid taking your life in your hands by attempting to cross the main road. Thankfully, such extreme measures are not needed today. There are many old pubs that used to be coaching inns for the last change of horses before Oxford. The attractive row of thatched cottages used to be one building, a malthouse where barley was prepared for brewing.

13. At a lane turn left.

A substantial town, Dorocina, grew up around the Roman fort. Some 13 acres were enclosed by stone walls that apparently were still standing in the 12th century. Since there is a shortage of suitable building stone in this area, perhaps they were used to build the abbey. The town outside the walls extended to approximately a further 60 acres. Some of this settlement was on the site now occupied by the allotments.

14. At some allotments on the left, turn right on a path signed 'Day's Lock ¾'. Walk across a field on a clear path then turn right in front of the Iron Age ramparts. Follow the path across a farm track until it ends in a field.

These substantial ramparts are known as Dyke Hills. They were built to secure the landward side of a piece of land bounded on two sides by the Thames and on the third by the Thame. The area thus enclosed provided a refuge for people and animals on this dangerous frontier.

15. Walk ahead to a bridge over the river. Cross the bridges and continue a short distance along the lane, back to the start.

Walk 19
PINKNEYS GREEN AND
MAIDENHEAD THICKET

The open, meadow-like expanse of Pinkneys Green and the heavily wooded Maidenhead Thicket both belong to the National Trust and provide a pleasing contrast for the two halves of this short, almost level walk. Maidenhead Thicket is perhaps at its most attractive in spring, when a mass of primroses bloom.

 The Old Shire Horse Centre was purpose-built by Courage Breweries in the mid 1970s to house the heavy horses that used to pull its drays and take part in parades, shows, pub openings and other events. The magnificent, 1-ton gentle giants have moved on to pastures new and, after lying empty for several years, the stables have been refurbished and reopened as a craft centre with a teashop. Coffee and Cream overlooks the

115

central courtyard and has several tables outside. They offer an excellent selection of really tempting cakes baked by a local lady and for lunch these are supplemented by a choice of sandwiches and baguettes, soup, ploughman's lunch or quiche and salad. They are open every day except Wednesday from 9.30 am until 5 pm. Telephone: 01628 828801.

When the tea shop is closed, both pubs passed en route - the Stag and Hounds at Pinkneys Green and the appropriately named Shire Horse next to the centre – both serve food.

DISTANCE: 3 miles.

MAP: OS Explorer 172 Chiltern Hills East.

STARTING POINT: National Trust car park at Pinkneys Green (GR 857809).

HOW TO GET THERE: From the Thicket Roundabout at the junction of the A4 and A404, take the A4 towards Maidenhead. At the next roundabout turn left on a minor road, signed 'Pinkneys Green' and 'Stubbings', to a car park about 300 yards ahead on the left.

ALTERNATIVE STARTING POINT: If you wish to visit the tea shop at the beginning or end of your walk, start at the Old Shire Horse Centre on the A4, where there is a large car park, though permission should be sought before leaving your car for a long period. You will then start the walk at point 9.

THE WALK

1. Facing the road take a path on the right of the car park. Ignore a path on the right leading to a footbridge over the A404 and follow the path through to the road by which you arrived at the car park. Go straight across and through a narrow belt of trees onto the common. Take a grassy path ahead across the common.

2. At the far side of the common turn left to walk along the right-hand side of the grassy expanse, ignoring all paths to the left and right, to a surfaced drive. Cross this and continue on a clear path ahead to a road.

3. Turn right for 50 yards and then turn left past the Stag and Hounds.

4. Turn left along a track called Bix Lane which soon narrows to a path leading to a lane. Go across this and follow a path along the right-hand side of the common. At a path junction by a house on the right, continue in the same direction to a junction in front of a large house called Leigh Cottage. Turn left to a road.

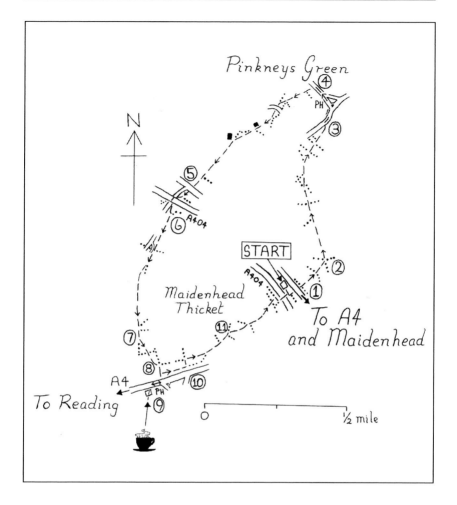

The name Pinkneys Green comes from a Norman knight, Ghilo de Pinkney, who was awarded land in this area as a reward for his support of William the Conqueror. The last Pinkney to be lord of the manor was Catherine Pinkney whose illegitimate son was adopted as heir of the Hoby estates at Bisham (see walk 8). Pinkneys Green's main claim to fame is that it was the birthplace of the Girl Guides, the first troop being formed here by Miss Baden-Powell in 1910.

5. Cross the road and follow the path down to a drive, ignoring a path on the left. Turn left under the A404 and then immediately bear left again, following the signed path up away from the drive.

117

Pinkneys Green.

6. At the top of the rise turn right. Follow the path ahead at a junction by some gates. When the path forks after about 100 yards, bear right to walk just inside the wood with a fence on the right and ignoring paths on the left.

7. More or less as the field on the right ends, bear left on the main path. Cross one wide path and continue to a second.

8. Turn right to a main road; the Old Shire Horse Centre with its tea room is across the road to the right, beyond the Shire Horse pub and through the car park.

9. Retrace your steps across the main road and now turn right on a path parallel with the road, just inside the wood, for 160 yards.

10. Opposite the end of Cherry Garden Lane turn left into the wood. After 50 yards turn right at a cross path for about $1/4$ mile, watching for a hollow or pit on the right.

This area is known as Maidenhead Thicket and along with the common land at Pinkneys Green is now owned by the National Trust. It was a favourite haunt of highwaymen who used this wild land as cover to prey on coaches. There is a record as early as 1255 of the vegetation being cut back to make passage safer. The vicar of Hurley was paid extra to brave the dangers of the thicket on his way to take services at Maidenhead. The romantically-named Robin Hood's arbour is a pen for animals which used to graze here. The various excavations have also revealed a potter's field with 11 kilns and other finds include a Palaeolithic hand axe.

11. Some 60 yards after the hollow, bear right at a fork (not a path on the right about 20 yards before the fork). Continue ahead as a path joins on the left. As you approach the A404 again, the traffic noise becomes more intrusive. Cross one major path and come to a T-junction with a second. Turn right and bear left after 25 yards to the footbridge over the A404 and back to the start.

Walk 20
GODSTOW AND OXFORD

For those who like walking beside water, this level walk is a must. The outward leg is beside the Thames, all the time heading towards the skyline of Oxford with its dreaming spires. The return is by the Oxford Canal. This route takes you right into the centre of the historic city, passing the starting point for walking and bus tours, so this walk could easily be combined with a visit to Oxford, avoiding the city's notorious traffic and parking problems.

 There is every sort of eating establishment in Oxford, including Mongolian! The best bet for a traditional English afternoon tea is the Ashmolean Museum cafe. It is under the museum but despite that is very light, airy and spacious. Both cakes and savoury food are available all day including the Stilton Challenge sandwich - Stilton, bacon and watercress on walnut bread with pear butter. A selection of delicious cakes is displayed and cream teas with clotted cream are served. Tasty lunches are available from 12 noon until 2 pm. The cafe is open every day except Monday from 10 am until 5 pm. Telephone: 01865 288183.

DISTANCE: 6 miles.
MAP: OS Explorer 180 Oxford.
STARTING POINT: Port Meadow car park, Wolvercote (GR 487094).
HOW TO GET THERE: From the Wolvercote roundabout in north Oxford at the junction of the A40 and A44 take the exit signed 'Wolvercote'. Follow this road for just under a mile through Wolvercote to a car park on the left.
ALTERNATIVE STARTING POINT: If you wish to visit the teashop at the beginning or end of your walk, start in Oxford, using one of the car parks or the park and ride, and make your way to the Ashmolean Museum. You will then start the walk at point 7.

THE WALK
1. Return to the road and turn left, passing the Trout Inn and crossing the bridge over the river Thames.

The delightful Trout Inn started life as the guest house of Godstow Nunnery, the remains of which are passed shortly. It overlooks the weir where shoals of chub grow fat on titbits. The first lock was built here in 1788 and the bridge over the navigation stream dates from that time. The bridge over the weir stream is older; one of its arches, the pointed one, is medieval.

2. Immediately over the bridge, turn left along the Thames Path, signed 'Osney 2½'.

Godstow Nunnery was a Benedictine house founded in 1133. It was heavily endowed by the Norman aristocracy whose widows and spinsters found this a comfortable retreat. Among them was Rosamund Clifford, mistress of Henry II, who retired here when he was forced to part from her under pressure from Queen Eleanor. She died in 1176 and her shrine scandalously became a place of pilgrimage. This was only one of many scandals associated with the nunnery, as the records of successive episcopal visitations show. The nuns were well known for their hospitality to the students from Oxford and repeated edicts enjoined the nuns to behave themselves in a more religious fashion. At the visitation by Bishop Alnwick in 1445, the Abbess complained that she could do nothing to stop it and was told to sleep in the dormitory with the nuns and to get up for matins with the sisters. The end came with the Dissolution in 1541 and the building was finally destroyed in the Civil War. What we see today are the outer walls and the shell of the abbess's private chapel.

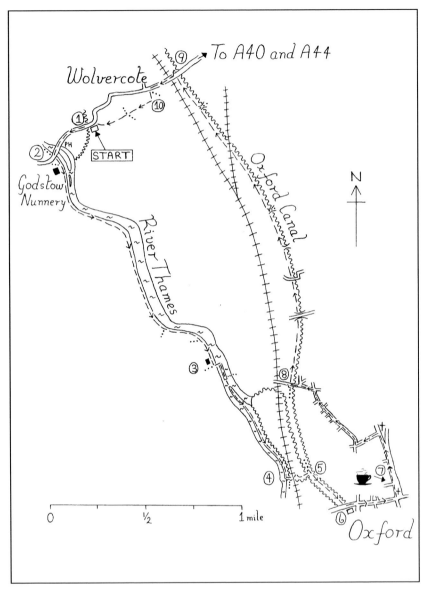

To A40 and A44

Wolvercote

Oxford Canal

River Thames

Godstow
Nunnery

N

START

PH

Godstow
Nunnery

0   ½   1 mile

Oxford

On 4 July 1862 a party rowed out from Oxford and had a picnic somewhere on this stretch of the river. Among them were Charles Dodgson, an Oxford mathematician and cleric better known as Lewis Carroll, and young Alice Lidell. From the stories told that day grew 'Alice in Wonderland'.

The remains of Godstow Nunnery.

3. At Bossom's Boatyard, cross a footbridge. Continue ahead, crossing a second bridge onto an island rather than a bridge on the left to the other side of the river. Soon the path lies on a kind of causeway with water on both sides.

4. When the path approaches houses, do not cross a bridge on the right but bear round to the left, signed 'Oxford Canal'. Pass under a very low railway bridge and continue on the path ahead to a bridge over another branch of the river to the canal bank at Isis Lock.

5. Cross the bridge (number 243) and turn right to follow the path between the canal on the left and the river on the right.

☕ **6.** At the end of the canal, go up to a road and turn left. At some traffic lights, continue in the same direction along George Street. At the end turn left along Magdalen Street to the Ashmolean Museum and tea room on the left on the corner of Beaumont Street.

Oxford lies on a bank of gravel in a bowl of hills, hemmed in by rivers so that, as this walk shows, the countryside penetrates right into the city. It is rather like a star with a long thin arm pointing north and fatter arms in the other directions. Its situation is said to lead to rheumatism and the Romans passed it by, preferring Dorchester to the south (see walk 18). With little room to expand, the only way to build was by pulling down first and so the centre of Oxford is crammed with fascinating buildings from every period of history though the street plan has hardly changed in a thousand years. There is so much to see it is well worth taking a guided tour by bus or on foot starting from the Tourist Information Centre, reached from George Street (telephone: 01865 726871). This short walk passes close to the site of the execution of the Protestant martyrs Latimer, Ridley and Cranmer in the 16th century, St Michael's, the oldest building in Oxford where Shakespeare once stood godfather, and the site of Beaumont Palace where Richard the Lionheart was born. The latter was where Beaumont Street now stands, which with St John Street is the only complete Georgian development in Oxford. On the corner is the Ashmolean Museum with its excellent cafe beneath. It was named after Elias Ashmole who inherited a collection of curiosities from one John Tradescant, son of Charles I's gardener, which he gave to the University. The building was completed in 1845.

7. After tea, continue in the same direction along St Giles. Turn left down Little Clarendon Street and then right along Walton Street. Turn left down Walton Well Road to reach the canal again. Cross a bridge over the canal.

St Giles is the patron saint of beggars and lepers and churches dedicated to him often lie outside city walls; here the church is just beyond the original north gate of the city. It is the widest street in the city and during the Civil War Charles I drilled his troops here. In the 16th century it became fashionable for wealthy merchants to move out of the crowded city centre and some of the buildings date from that time. A fair is still held every September.

8. Turn left down to the towpath. Turn left under the bridge you have just crossed. Walk along the towpath for about 2 miles to Wolvercote Lock, the first lock.

One of the first canals to be constructed in England, the Oxford Canal aimed to connect the industry of the Midlands with London via the Thames. Royal assent was given in April 1769 and work began in Coventry in September. Financial problems meant it took 20 years to reach Oxford and it was officially opened in 1790. Previously coal had been brought to the city from Newcastle by sea and the Thames; now it could come more directly and within days the price had dropped dramatically. It was initially a great success though first the opening of the Grand Union Canal and then the railway took away its traffic. In the 1950s it was threatened with closure but saved after an energetic campaign and it is a popular leisure canal today.

9. Leave the towpath and go up some steps on the left to a road. Turn right.

10. Just before the first house on the left, turn left through a gate onto the common, signed as a bridleway. Do not take the obvious track half left but bear right, skirting round some gardens and then walking parallel with them to a gate onto the road next to the car park where this walk started.

Port Meadow has belonged to the Freemen of Oxford for over a thousand years. It has been grazed and mown for hay since the Bronze Age and never ploughed or sprayed with chemicals, so it is of considerable ecological significance.